Superpower, China?

Historicizing Beijing's New Narratives of Leadership and East Asia's Response Thereto

World Scientific – Now Publishers Series in Business: **Vol.6**

Superpower, China?

Historicizing Beijing's New Narratives of Leadership and East Asia's Response Thereto

Niv Horesh
The University of Nottingham, UK

Hyun Jin Kim
The University of Melbourne, Australia

Peter Mauch
University of Western Sydney, Australia

now

World Scientific

Published by

World Scientific Publishing Co. Pte. Ltd.

5 Toh Tuck Link, Singapore 596224

USA office: 27 Warren Street, Suite 401-402, Hackensack, NJ 07601

UK office: 57 Shelton Street, Covent Garden, London WC2H 9HE

and

now publishers Inc.
PO Box 1024
Hanover, MA 02339
USA

Library of Congress Cataloging-in-Publication Data
Horesh, Niv.
Superpower, China? : historicizing Beijing's new narratives of leadership and East Asia's response thereto / by Niv Horesh (The University of Nottingham, UK), Hyun Jin Kim (The University of Melbourne, Australia), Peter Mauch (University of Western Sydney, Australia).
pages cm. -- (World Scientific-now publishers series in business, ISSN 2251-3442 ; Vol. 6)
Includes bibliographical references and index.
ISBN 978-9814619158
1. China--Politics and government--2002– 2. China--Foreign relations. 3. China--Foreign economic relations. 4. China--Foreign relations--East Asia. 5. East Asia--Foreign relations--China. I. Kim, Hyun Jin, 1982– II. Mauch, Peter (Peter Cameron) III. Title.
DS779.46.H66 2015
327.5105--dc23

2014028673

British Library Cataloguing-in-Publication Data
A catalogue record for this book is available from the British Library.

In-house Editors: Sandhya Venkatesh/Chitralekha Elumalai

Typeset by Stallion Press
Email: enquiries@stallionpress.com

Printed in Singapore by B & Jo Enterprise Pte Ltd

Contents

About the Authors

Niv Horesh is a Professor (Chair) in the Modern History of China and Director of the China Policy Institute at the University of Nottingham. Horesh has worked in the past as a Business Development Manager in China, and as a civil servant in Israel and Australia. He is the author of *Chinese Money in Global Context* (Stanford University Press, 2013).

Hyun Jin Kim is a Lecturer in Classics in the Discipline of Classics and Archaeology at the University of Melbourne, Australia. He is the author of *Ethnicity and Foreigner in Ancient Greece and China* (2009, Duckworth) and *The Huns, Rome and the Birth of Europe* (Cambridge University Press, 2013).

Peter Mauch is a Senior Lecturer in International History at the University of Western Sydney (Australia). He has authored numerous books on Asian history, including *Sailor Diplomat: Nomura Kichisaburo and the Japanese–American War* (Harvard University Press, 2011).

Introduction

Soon after the turn of the 21st century, American political scientist Kenneth Waltz wrote simply and matter-of-factly about China's upward trajectory. "China will emerge as a great power even without trying very hard", he noted, "so long as it remains politically united and competent".[1] Setting aside the question as to whether or not China has tried very hard in the ensuing decade, it has indeed maintained its domestic political stability and has continued its breathtaking rise. Much is attributable to the Chinese economy. It is today the world's second-largest economy (having overtaken Japan in mid-2010). It is the world's largest trading economy, the world's second-largest destination of foreign direct investment, and the world's largest holder of foreign exchange reserves. It is also the largest manufacturer on the globe. This economic success has meant expendable income, and China is spending on another key indicator of great power status: the military. Even allowing for the large (presumed) gap between China's official defense budget and its actual defense spending, China's defense budget is second only to the United States. It also occupies a privileged position in world politics, courtesy of its permanent seat on the United Nations Security Council. Its increasing diplomatic confidence has become readily apparent in recent years, and it has proved willing to "use its veto power to constrain, shape, and sometimes derail the proposals of others,

[1] K. N. Waltz, "Structural Realism after the Cold War", in G. John Ikenberry (ed.), *America Unrivaled: The Future of the Balance of Power* (Ithaca, NY: Cornell University Press, 2002), p. 56.

including the USA…".[2] Economically, militarily, and diplomatically, China is rising.

The world is watching China's rise with a mix of wonder, curiosity, fear, and even jealousy. All around the globe, academicians, financial experts, journalists, elite-level policy-makers, defense personnel, and laypersons alike puzzle over China's rise, and what it portends for the world. Will China rise peacefully? *Can* it rise peacefully? Is China on a collision course with the United States? Must China's rise go hand-in-hand with US decline? Is China's behavior toward its nearest neighbors indicative of a growing Chinese truculence? Or, was former leader Hu Jintao closer to the mark with his avowals of China's peaceful rise? Will China's stunning economic growth continue? Might a preponderance of Chinese economic power mean that other nations become dependent on China for their own economic health? Might China seek to use such economic leverage and pile the political pressure on economically-dependent nations? Will greater economic clout among China's fast-growing middle class result in demands for greater political freedom? What will become of the divide between China's urban middle classes and the rural poor? What happens if (when?) the Chinese economy slows down? Will the Chinese Communist Party prove able to maintain its legitimacy?[3]

Questions such as these abound. Their individual and collective worth is self-evident. Such questions nonetheless leave certain issues unaddressed

---

[2]For a detailed examination of the Chinese economy, see W. M. Morrison, "China's Economic Rise: History, Trends, Challenges, and Implications for the United States", Congressional Research Service (CRS) Report, February 3, 2014. Available at: https://www.fas.org/sgp/crs/row/RL33534.pdf. (All cited websites were re-accessed on January 3, 2011, in order to verify their content.) Concerning China's use of the veto on the UN Security Council, see J. Wuthnow, *Chinese Diplomacy and the United Nations Security Council: Beyond the Veto* (London: Routledge, 2013), p. 8.

[3]These questions receive treatment in B. Buzan (2010). "China in International Society: Is 'Peaceful Rise' Possible?", *Chinese Journal of International Politics*, 3(1): 5–36; J. J. Mearsheimer (2006). "China's Unpeaceful Rise", *Current History*, 105(690): 160–162; J. R. Itzkowitz Shifrinson and M. Beckley (2012). "Correspondence: Debating China's Rise and U.S. Decline", *International Security*, 37(3) (Winter): 172–181; A. J. Tellis, T. Tanner, and J. Keough, *Strategic Asia 2011–2012: Asia Responds to its Rising Powers, China and India* (Seattle: National Bureau of Asian Research, 2011); X. Li and V. Worm (2011). "Building China's Soft Power for a Peaceful Rise", *Journal of Chinese Political Science*, 16(1) (March): 69–89; and H. White (2011). "Power Shift: Rethinking Australia's Place in the Asian Century", *Australian Journal of International Affairs*, 65(1): 81–93.

and unresolved. For one thing, these questions invite little or no historical contextualization. Nor, for that matter, do they necessarily probe whatever it is that China might bring to the table as a great power. The question as to how the Chinese view their own nation's trajectory remains unaddressed. And, the popular reactions of China's near neighbors in South Korea and Japan remain relatively little studied. It is precisely these issues to which the following chapters address themselves; each issue receives brief treatment in this introduction.

Historicizing China's Rise

How might China's rise best be understood? Might historical context provide insights? To many, the answer to the second question will necessarily be affirmative. To those for whom the answer is anything but self-evident, it perhaps makes sense to quote historians Ernest May and Richard Neustadt, who have argued: "One of history's uses is to understand people whose age, sex, race, nationality, or beliefs are different from one's own". May and Neustadt also suggested that "history can stimulate imagination" and that "seeing the past can help one envision alternative futures".[4] In the context of these observations, it seems fair to assert that historicizing China's rise provides — at the very least — one way of understanding China's current trajectory.

This leads to another question: To which historical precedent should one turn? Did Japanese Prime Minister Abe Shinzo get it right when he recently likened the contemporary Sino-Japanese relationship to that of Germany and Britain on the eve of World War I? Is Harvard Law School's Noah Feldman correct in his assertion that China and the United States are on the verge not of a Cold War but of a "Cool War", in which a "classic struggle for power is unfolding at the same time as economic cooperation is becoming deeper…".[5] It might also prove instructive to go back further in time. In this context, it is well to recall what most Chinese

[4]E. R. May and R. E. Neustadt, *Thinking in Time: The Uses of History for Decision-Makers* (New York: Free Press, 1986), pp. xiii, xv.

[5]"Echoing the Guns of August: China, Japan, and the First World War", *The Economist*, January 23, 2014. Available at: http://www.economist.com/blogs/banyan/2014/01/china-japan-and-first-world-war. N. Feldman, *Cool War: The Future of Global Competition* (New York: Random House, 2013), p. xii.

regard as axiomatic. "The most obvious point that can be made about the rise of Chinese power in the twenty-first century", according to long-time Sinologist Warren I. Cohen, "is that it is a *resurrection* rather than a new or unique phenomenon".[6]

China as a Great Power, and Chinese Views of Their Nation's Rise

How will China behave as a Great Power? How will it leave its imprint on world politics? Needless to say, there are almost as many answers to this question as there are scholars willing to offer those answers. One or two things seem certain: (1) China is (or will be) a driver of the transition from a unipolar, post-Cold War world order to whatever emerges in its place, and (2) the Sino-American relationship will be one of the key determinants of the new world order.

Working from these twin assumptions, Chapters 2–4 probe both Western (particularly American) and Chinese scholarship for insights. A few salient points immediately present themselves. First, despite talk of a "Washington consensus" and a "Beijing consensus" (or, alternative pathways to Great Power status) there is, in fact, *no* consensus concerning the nature of the world that is emerging. Among the manifold uncertainties and variables is that relating to China's behavior. How might China's path to modernity best be explained? And does that path provide any pointers as to China's post-modern future?

Many have offered opinions on this issue. Whether the proffered opinions take heed of the rich intellectual milieu within which Chinese academics and policymakers operate is, however, altogether another matter. In other words, the question as to how the Chinese view their nation's trajectory remains, all too often, unaddressed. This has negative consequences for our understanding of China. To borrow the words of the Japanese daily, *Asahi Shimbun Globe*: "We need to understand China as it

[6]"Echoing the Guns of August: China, Japan, and the First World War", *The Economist*, January 23, 2014. Available at: http://www.economist.com/blogs/banyan/2014/01/china-japan-and-first-world-war. N. Feldman, *Cool War: The Future of Global Competition* (New York: Random House, 2013), p. xii. W. I. Cohen, "China's Rise in Historical Perspective", in Q. Zhao and G. Liu (eds.), *Managing the China Challenge: Global Perspectives* (London: Routledge, 2009), p. 23 (*italics added*).

is, not as we want it to be".[7] For this very reason, this book gives sustained, critical attention to the works of Wang Hui and Yan Xuetong, both of whom seek answers to China's future in its significant past.

The Northeast Asian Neighborhood

Another significant body of thought concerning China's rise emanates from its near Northeast Asian neighbors in South Korea and Japan. Nonetheless, the language barrier is such that Western readers have limited access to South Korean and Japanese reactions to China's rise. English-language scholarship is, moreover, overwhelmingly concerned with official Japanese and/or South Korean policy toward China (and vice versa). Readers may well be familiar with, to cite but one prominent example, the ongoing Sino-Japanese spat over the Senkaku–Daioyu Islands.

By the same token, readers may well be less familiar with popularly expressed nationalisms in China, Japan, and South Korea. Chapter 5 uses the renaming of Seoul in the Chinese language as a conceptual lens through which to view the interactions and intersections of nationalistic thought in Northeast Asia. The resulting portrait defies easy characterization. Suffice it here to note that the long heritage shared by China, Korea, and Japan — symbolized, in this instance, by the Chinese writing system — does not necessarily provide for greater regional understanding. Nor, for that matter, does a shared mistrust of China among South Korean and Japanese policy-makers pave the way for greater levels of understanding between those two nations and their peoples. This is a major theme to emerge in both Chapters 5 and 6. Perhaps most interestingly, these two chapters point to (particularly) South Korea as a bellwether of China's future regional leadership ambitions.

The Structure and Arguments of the Book

We begin exploring these issues by offering a detailed survey of two important recent books: *Rome and China* and *Life Under Pressure*.[8] In

[7] "We Need to Understand China as it is, not as we want it to be", November 8, 2013, *Asahi Shimbun Globe*. Available at: https://ajw.asahi.com/article/globe/economy/AJ201311080016.

[8] W. Scheidel (ed.), *Rome and China: Comparative Perspectives on Ancient World Empires* (USA: Oxford University Press, 2011); T. Bengtsson, C. Campbell and J. Z. Lee, *Life Under Pressure* (Cambridge, MA: The MIT Press, 2004).

tandem, these books problematize Western perceptions about Chinese history, and China's position on the world stage in pre-modern times. We thereby seek to historicize contemporary Chinese power; here we are concerned with the questions of whether China should be seen as emergent, resurgent, or profoundly divergent; and the extent to which the path it has charted can be deemed exceptional.

Chapter 2 then discussed how, once the rise of China is placed within a historical context, scholars have been attempting to deconstruct the nature of the "China Model" that has helped propel China once the course of the last three decades. How unique is this "Model"? And does putative uniqueness mean China will change the international system in new meaningful ways?

Can the "China Model" be defined and is it exportable? The answers offered are varied and complex, ranging from a defense of the much-maligned Washington consensus and attempts to explain the "China Model" within that consensus to an enthusiastic argument for the propagation of the so-called "Beijing consensus" *in lieu* of the old Washington consensus. The essence of this debate however is, as can be expected, the specter of China posing a challenge to the current US global hegemony. That possibility or eventuality however is arguably dependent not just on economic developments but also the attitudes toward China of key regional players in the East Asia region, namely Korea and Japan.

Before examining the perception of China's rise and its impact among China's East Asian neighbors however, the Chinese analysis of their own economic success will be scrutinized in Chapter 3. With the perceived "decline" of US power very much in focus, Chinese intellectuals such as Wang Hui have advocated neo-Maoist views in opposition to American neo-liberalism and its Chinese liberal adherents. It was observed how an intellectual battle is being fought in today's China to determine what kind of state a rising China should be. The arguments touch the essence of what exactly should constitute the "China Model".

Chapter 4 then moves on to discuss the versatility of Chinese internal debate on the future trajectory of this "China Model", with particular focus on the work of Yan Xuetong. It observes how Yan Xuetong seeks to articulate China's moral claim to global leadership by drawing inspiration from China's ancient classical literature and philosophy, particularly Xunzi. We consequently aim to explore the extent to which Yan's sense of Chinese pre-modern history is valid, and whether pre-modern prescripts genuinely inform modern Chinese policy.

Assuming China is as genuinely and historically war-averse as it nowadays claims to be, can China win over the rest of the world through "soft war"? The episode of the renaming of South Korea's capital in Chinese, discussed in Chapter 5, is particularly instructive in this regard. It will observe how the PRC government reacted with prudence to the South Korean requests for the name-change with little jingoism or attempts at confrontation. China's leaders and diplomats *on this occasion* exhibited the kind of diplomatic maturity and statesmanship befitting an aspirant for global leadership. More recent escalation of disputes between China and its neighbors across the East China and South China seas has since all but relegated the re-naming of Seoul in Chinese to a footnote. We believe, nevertheless, that the re-naming episode was undeservedly overlooked by scholars.

The last chapter examines how China's rise and increasing tensions with Japan are portrayed by South Korean bloggers. The deterioration in relations between China and Japan over the last two years generally projects on to the ways and means by which China's rise is portrayed in South Korea. Since Korea's relations with both its more populous neighbors have been historically fraught, and since it is also implicated in various territorial disputes with both countries, determining Korean sensibilities is an important way of gaging shifts in public opinion across the region. Although the conservative political establishments in both South Korea and Japan might see China as a constant threat, South Korean and Japanese netizens still popularly view each other with suspicion. By contrast, we conclude that popular perceptions of the China threat in either South Korea or Japan may be swayed in the future if there is an escalation of the territorial disputes that these two US allies still have with one another, or in case North Korea implodes.

Chapter 1

Was There a Pre-Modern or Early-Modern "China Model"?

In a 1965 article entitled "The State of Economic History", Douglass North suggested that improvements in economic organization might have been "as important as technological change in the development of the Western world between 1500 and 1830". Although students of American economic history had drawn "broad inferences from scraps of evidence [about] the relationship between the money supply, price levels, and specie flows", most economic historians working at the time were oblivious to incidence theory, and in some cases, spurned systematic quantitative analysis altogether. On the whole, North castigated much of the research in the field — then still heavily weighted toward the West — as much less as rigorous than the work done by economists.[1]

Over the next four decades, a "New Economic History" emerged whereby one segment of the field has championed "cliometrics" in order to keep abreast with advances in quantitative techniques that are used to research contemporary economies. But in some instances, such measuring techniques were lapped up at the expense of broader social contexture and in the face of lingering doubts about the representativeness or reliability of pre-20th century quantitative data. Cliometricians have come under fire not only for that but also for their espousal of neo-classical reductionism which — contrary to North's own research agenda — eventually lapsed into understating the complex role played by institutions in welfare-enhancement

[1]D. C. North (1965). "The State of Economic History", *American Economic Review*, 55(1–2): 86–91.

and the interplay between technological innovation, property rights, and path dependency.[2]

Through much of the 1980s and early 1990s, it seemed that the divisions between "hard" and "soft" economic-history research was widening due to greater specialization over time. The contours and rationale of articles appearing in *Explorations in Economic History* thus began looking increasingly different to the ones published, for example, in *Business History*. In the former journal, regressions have patently become an indispensable touchstone for academic rigor, whereas a few other journals still occasionally allowed for narrative detail and historic context to take center-stage. At the same time, economists and historians seemed to have engaged one another's findings less frequently, with those working on the intersection of history and economics often finding refuge in area-studies departments. The growing divisions between economists' work and that of great many economic historians, as well as the latter's loss of prestige, meant that a number of universities shut down their once fiercely-independent departments of economic history, relegating staff to either retirement, or to playing second fiddle in management schools.

It was not until the mid-1990s that economic historians had come into vogue again on the back of globalization. Suddenly, there was great urgency to understand better the historic trajectories defining East and West, and speculations based on the lessons of history concerning a possible decline in Western hegemony found many new listeners. Certainly, the recent Global Financial Crisis has amplified the spectre of a 21st "Asian" or "Chinese Century" led by interventionist governments, namely, governments which by and large reject neo-classical prescripts. This turnaround called on academics to go beyond the now somewhat eclipsed

---

[2]M. Kipping and B. Üsdiken, "Business History and Management Studies", in G. Jones and J. Zeitlin (eds.), *The Oxford Handbook of Business History* (Oxford: Oxford University Press, 2007), pp. 103, 109; N. R. Lamoreaux, D. M. Raff, and P. Temin, "Economic Theory and Business History", in G. Jones and J. Zeitlin (eds.), *The Oxford Handbook of Business History* (Oxford: Oxford University Press, 2007). See also O'Brien's ambivalent retrospective tribute P. K. O'Brien, "Afterword: The Shock, Achievements and Disappointments of the New", in J. S. Lyons, L. P. Cain, and S. H. Williamson (eds.), *Reflections on the Cliometrics Revolution: Conversations with Economic Historians* (London: Routledge, 2008).

neo-classical consensus about the healing, timeless powers of the market in order to provide lessons from similar regulatory crises in the past.

Against this backdrop, the late-1990s also saw the rise of another important vein of literature, mostly (but not only) among economic historians of a narrative bent: the "California School". Pomeranz's *Great Divergence* is arguably the most influential study in this vein; it has stimulated scholars to re-think East–West historic binaries, and question the foundations as well as the duration of Western economic and technological supremacy.[3] Contrary to what the title of his path-breaking book might suggest, however, Pomeranz cast in fact very serious doubts on the notion that northwest Europe had achieved unparalleled affluence or displayed a more sophisticated economic organization than East Asian polities anytime before the late-18th century.

The debate between proponents of the California School and their critics has in the last few years spread into many new areas of exploration, e.g., comparative literature, postcolonial studies, price theory, and implicitly even into environmental conservation.[4] However, a detailed survey of the debate and the disciplines it is beginning to touch on is beyond the scope of this introductory chapter. Instead, I aim to critique below two collaborative research projects that, when read in tandem, significantly re-define the temporal dimensions of the debate; both involved leading experts and produced edited volumes infused with — somewhat uncharacteristically of this genre — wonderfully consistent internal logic. I will then place these two volumes within the broader sweep of recently-published comparative histories, and diachronically underscore their relevance to China's current economic reform thrust.

[3] K. Pomeranz, *The Great Divergence: China, Europe, and the Making of the Modern World Economy* (Princeton, NJ: Princeton University Press, 2000).

[4] See, e.g., J. M. Hobson, *The Eastern Origin of Western Civilization* (Cambridge: Cambridge University Press, 2004); C. H. Shiue and W. Keller (2004). "Markets in China and Europe on the Eve of the Industrial Revolution". National Bureau of Economic Research Working Paper 10778; R. Markley, *The Far East and the English Imagination, 1600–1730* (Cambridge: Cambridge University Press, 2006); N. Horesh (2008). "Silk, Tea, and Treasure: Maritime Trade in Eighteenth-Century Literature", *Sungkyun Journal of East Asian Studies*, 8(2): 131–142; on environmental conservation, see e.g., J. Diamond, *Collapse: How Societies Choose to Fail or Succeed* (New York: Viking, 2005).

Going Pre-1700s Is Instructive

Edited by Professor Walter Scheidel of Stanford University, *Rome and China* might be the swallow auguring the imminent demise of the regionally-compartmentalized discourse on ancient history. Already, "Global" or "World History" is fast becoming a buzzword in job advertisement for early-modern and modern history academic positions irrespective of the regional specialization sought after. Here, Walter Scheidel aims much earlier, namely, to whittle down any lingering divisions between scholars once dubbed "classicists" and those dubbed "orientalists". He assembles four Greco-Roman scholars (including himself) and two Sinologists working on different periods, and tasks them with offering their thoughts on the "First Great Divergence" between the Eastern and Western *ecumene*. As a justification for this study, Scheidel rightly posits that (p. 6) ". . . although some explicitly comparative work on China and the Mediterranean in antiquity has appeared in recent years, it is very heavily weighted in favor of intellectual history" rather than socioeconomic history.

The contributors oblige with compelling insights, though some readers might note the underlying tentative tenor of this pioneering project and the inherent limitations of some of data that is drawn upon. The first and last chapters have been authored by Scheidel himself. Titled "From the Great Convergence to the First Great Divergence", Chapter 1 seeks to stylize the Roman vs. Han polity. It questions whether geography or climate can exclusively account for China's extraordinary political unity over the last two millennia compared with the political fragmentation of the Mediterranean basin. If anything, one might expect that western Eurasia, where maritime links were much more extensive, would show greater political and ideational integration (p. 12).

Scheidel adds to the broader picture socio-cultural factors such as the comparatively loose linkage between ideology and administrative power in Rome as opposed to the Confucian-Legalist ethos pervading state authority in Qin-Han China. Perhaps for that reason, the power of the warrior class in China ". . . was mostly contained", a relatively large civilian bureaucracy emerged and there was less reliance on slave labor (pp. 17–19).[5] Scheidel

[5]On the significance of slavery in classical Greece as opposed to Han China, see also G. Lloyd and N. Sivin, *The Way and the Word: Science and Medicine in Early China and Greece* (New Haven: Yale University Press, 2002), Chapters 2 and 3.

then marshals secondary sources to suggest that, by 400 CE, the Roman empire had employed 30,000 civilian officials, compared to around four times as many in Western Han China (206 BC–9 CE).

This observation is, of course, of value because the early-modern (i.e., "Second") Great Divergence appear to have entailed an inverse ratio between the percentage of civil servants in the overall population of Britain, and the percentage of mandarins and bailiffs in the overall Chinese population. Echoing Max Weber, Scheidel then posits that an even more significant difference between the Roman and the early Chinese empires lay in the fact that Han cities did not have self-governing councils or elections and were thus much weaker compared with the enduring Mediterranean city-state modality.

Penned by Nathan Rosenstein, Chapter 2 deals with war and military institutions as determinants of state formations (pp. 24–51). Rosenstein concludes that, in comparison to China, Roman military hegemony was "... in general not oppressive" because it was more reliant on colonies and allies' assent. In return for placing their military forces at Rome's disposal, colonies and allies were left almost entirely autonomous (p. 30). Chapter 3 by Karen Turner (pp. 52–82) surveys the legal divergence between Latin civil law and China's essentially punitive code. Contrary to popular perceptions about China's legal system, her article does not portray early-imperial sentences as more cruel than the ones meted out by Roman magistrates.[6] However, Turner does believe that Roman legal proceedings were systematically more balanced, allowing "alternative voices" to speak in defense of commoners accused by the state of wrong-doing. Equally important, it also allowed for greater freedom for women.

Chapter 4 by Maria H. Dettenhofer (pp. 83–99) provides an interesting brief overview of eunuchism. At the end of the 1st century CE, Rome unlike China forbade castration on its soil, but eunuchs from overseas (mostly slaves or ex-slaves) continued to be in high demand. Overall, eunuchs seem to have been historically much more powerful and numerous at the Chinese imperial court where even strong emperors were subject to

[6]The perception of a rapaciously autocratic China may have been entrenched by K. A. Wittfogel, *Oriental Despotism: A Comparative Study of Total Power* (New Haven, CT: Yale University Press, 1957), who did not pay sufficient attention to the diminution of the state bureaucracy in the late-imperial era.

their influence. Turner then contends that most Chinese emperors were in fact bisexual, presumably because they grew up sheltered from the outside world by eunuchs (p. 88). Although not explicitly discussed in this chapter, Dettenhofer's contention does bring to mind famous 16th–18th century Jesuit observations about the pervasiveness of "sodomy" in China as compared with Europe.[7]

Chapter 5 by Peter Fibiger Bang (pp. 100–120) focuses on tributary trade. Bang's proposition is that it played much bigger role in shaping China's foreign relations than in Rome, where the state did not intervene in the economy to the same extent (corvée labor, for example, was apparently less common in the latter). He also quite plausibly speculates that "buying and selling of land" played a bigger role in Rome, because property rights were more clearly defined there. Chapter 6 by Mark Edward Lewis (pp. 121–136) juxtaposes the religious and euergentist foundations of the Western notion of charity with the Chinese emphasis on imperially-regulated famine relief through the maintenance of statewide granaries. These reflect again what may perhaps be loosely termed as the "urban bias" of the West: in China, the religious establishment was eventually subsumed under state aegis, and cities were materially and conceptually "evanescent" (e.g., built from wood rather than stone, and administered by politically weak local elites and bailiffs).

Concluding this volume is an in-depth overview of the evolution of the Greco-Roman and Chinese coinage systems featuring highly illuminating sets of quantitative data (pp. 137–207). Here, Scheidel persuasively draws out the distinction between early-Imperial China's predominantly base-metal monetary system to the mineral riches available to Rome and to its higher-denomination silver-based currencies. If corroborated by further research, his incisive conclusion that "...the Roman empire was significantly more monetized than the Han state" (p. 205) might well re-make the way scholars conceive of, and date, the 'Great Divergence' between East and West. It might perhaps also shed some light on the distant origins of the credit economy, which distinguished northeast Europe from the rest of the World in the early-modern era.

---

[7]See e.g., J. D. Spence, *The Chan's Great Empire: China in Western Minds* (New York: Norton, 1999), pp. 23–38.

Going Households Is Revealing

If Scheidel's work might send scholars in search of a great divergence between the Western and East Asian pre-modern economies right back to the beginning of the Common Era, the Eurasia Research Project which yielded *Life Under Pressure* does not at first glance point to any dramatic divergence in life expectancy — and therefore no difference in living standards along geographical lines — before the early 19th century. Informed by California School precepts, the great bogey Bengtsson, Campbell, Lee, and their co-authors set out to defy in this edited volume is no other than the Malthusian notion that preventive demographic checks did not exist in East Asia. It does that by meticulously examining mortality rates in relation to the makeup of households and grain prices in rural communities ranging from Scania (near Lund, Sweden), through Sart (near Liège, Belgium), North Italy, and Ou (present-day Fukushima Prefecture, north-eastern Japan) to present-day Liaodong Province in China.

Despite its overall revisionist thrust, and somewhat surprisingly in tune with Karen Turner's chapter in the book reviewed above, *Life Under Pressure* suggests in fact that early-modern East Asian families were "... larger and more complex than West European families, their organization was more hierarchical and their resources more concentrated under the control of senior members" (p. 86); traditions of male dominance "... were arguably strongest in China and perhaps Japan and somewhat weaker in Belgium and Sweden" (p. 341); the average age of marriage and childbearing in East Asia was "... about five years younger" than in the European communities examined (p. 343). Indeed, readers who are by now mindful of a possibly much more ancient divergence between East and West might recall that Marco Polo himself lauded the chasteness of Chinese women as way of rebuking the promiscuity of Venetian women.[8]

Partly in tune with Mark Lewis' chapter, *Life Under Pressure* observes too that the praxis of charity in East Asia was distinct: it had a lot to do with the perceived obligation of the state to nourish the rural poor in times of famine, whereas it was the religious establishment which played an arguably commensurate role in the West. But that is not to say that state granaries

[8] *Ibid.*, pp. 15–18.

were not maintained to that end in the West at all. Surprisingly, the authors tell of a somewhat similar granary apparatus in early 19th century Sweden (pp. 140–141).

Multi-ethnicity, local custom, and hygienic awareness in each one of these communities surveyed, as well as the vast distances between some of them, would naturally militate against sweeping generalizations. In North Italy, for example, the authors tell of "subpopulations who shared the same or perhaps worse conditions from the socioeconomic and environmental point of view but enjoyed a much more favorable mortality regime. This was the case of the Jewish communities, whose infant mortality rate was around half of that of the Catholic population with which they lived, showing that cultural attitudes in child care and lifestyle could significantly overcome the mortality effects of external constraints" (pp. 212–213). Similarly, the authors explain that "... the most conservative part of the nineteenth-century Dutch Protestant church rejected vaccination against smallpox as an offence to God" (p. 391).[9]

Indeed, the authors carefully eschew the pitfall of macro-level generalities by foregrounding the internal dynamics of the household in each region. Yet, at least in one instance, the authors' own data might raise some questions about their overall argument. Table 3.1 (p. 66), for example, suggests that life expectancy (at the age of one) in Belgium might have already been considerably higher than in China or Japan in the 18th century (~52 in Belgium vs. ~47 and ~42 in China and Japan respectively). Admittedly, the life-expectancy gap is barely noticeable when East Asia is compared with the European economic periphery (i.e., North Italy) at that time. But readers would do well to bear in mind that the Asian data do not record the common incidence of female infanticide there (p. 68; *cf.* pp. 275–277, 337). In other words, the East Asian population cross-section in the dataset had been predisposed to live longer. And yet, it did not live as long as in Belgium or Sweden. By the same token, the authors suggest in passing that, in mid-18th century rural Belgium, roughly half the persons born would have survived to the age of 55, and around one-third to the age of 65. In rural northeast

[9]The lack of primogeniture was once cited as a cause for China's falling behind. But, interestingly, primogeniture was widely practiced in the Ou communities surveyed in *Life Under Pressure*, see p. 260.

China, only around one-third of the persons born would have survived to the age of 55, and only 20% to the age 65 (p. 410; *cf.* 426).

Chapter 10 (pp. 293–324) constitutes the revisionist core of this comparative work as it boldly aims to discard, along California School lines, the notion that China had lower standard of living than Europe before the 1800s. The authors of this chapter, Campbell and Lee, contend that "comparisons of mortality levels between China and Europe fail to reveal systematic differences indicative of lower living standards in the former. Adult mortality varied considerably within China and does not seem to have been consistently higher than that in historical European populations" (p. 295). Indeed, Table 10.1 (p. 276) shows estimates of life expectancy in China for males (calculated at age 10) varying between 48.4 in Liaodong and 33.5 in Taiwan throughout the pre-war era.

The authors' emphasis on local custom, religion, and ethnicity as determinants of life expectancy in Chapter 8 might problematize the degree to which the cross-section analyzed in Chapter 10 can be seen as representative of China. Following James Lee's previous work, Campbell and Lee highlight here communities of Han bannermen from Liaodong (the Qing Banners were also made up of non-Han combatants). These, we are told, ". . . were assigned to the Imperial Household agency and were closely monitored as they were Royal Peasants and of more concern to the imperial court than regular population" (p. 298). To be sure, imperially-bestowed privileges might have been partially offset by the risks that these bannermen's military occupation posed, but it would be difficult to accept that imperial favors and soldiery simply cancel out one another when it comes to inferring from the data mortality rates for the overall population (*cf.* p. 323).

The scarcity of reliable population data from the late-Imperial period often pre-determines researcher's regional focus. Liaodong, in that sense, would certainly be more representative of China than the highly-commercialized Yangzi delta. That said, Liaodong was part of the littoral economy, pivoted on the Yangzi delta, not part of the hinterland economy. It was an area that, in the authors' words, was ". . . heavily involved in coastal and, during the last half of the 19th century, international trade as well" (p. 300). One could add, moreover, that it was situated in close proximity to the Manchu historic heartland, and therefore particularly precious to the ruling Qing dynasty.

Living standards aside, *Life Under Pressure* offers other invaluable comparative observations about the 18th century across Eurasia that again bring to mind the much earlier period covered in *Rome and China*. Much like Lewis's chapter, *Life Under Pressure* concludes too that "... Western states organized to protect property at the expense of the poor, while Eastern states promoted stability even at the expense of the powerful. The socioeconomic gradient in mortality responses to economic stress was accordingly more pronounced in the West than in the East" (p. 432). Certainly, the institutional parallels one can draw here between antiquity and the early-modern era along the Eurasian faultline call for more research on not just the origins of either civilization but also on their respective permutation over time.

Taking the Debate Forward

Nearly two millennia separate the cased-studies analyzed by the two books under review in this chapter. Could it be that the some important pieces in the Great-Divergence jigsaw puzzle might be found mid-way through? Historians of Europe would quite naturally point to the Renaissance as the mainspring of Western modernity, but the period does not loom large in the debate between California School proponents and their critics. Similarly, our understanding of the level of proto-scientific knowledge in the non-West, and the ways in which it had nourished Renaissance thinkers is imperfect, though Joseph Needham's monumental project and Watt's pioneering study certainly made great strides in elucidating the mediating role of the Islamic world to that effect.[10]

In his recently-published *Financial History of the World*, Niall Ferguson too has drawn our attention to the fact that "... economic life in the Eastern world — in the Abassid Caliphate or in Song China — was far more advanced" at least until Fibonacci introduced Indian algebraic precepts in early 13th century Italy; these were later reified by the Medicis into double-entry bookkeeping in the Florentine republic.[11]

---

[10] J. Needham, *Science and Civilisation in China*. 6 vols (Cambridge: Cambridge University Press, 1954–1988); W. M. Watt, *The Influence of Islam on Medieval Europe* (Edinburgh: Edinburgh University Press, 1972).

[11] N. Ferguson, *Ascent of Money: A Financial History of the World* (New York: Penguin, 2008), pp. 32–43.

By the early 17th century, European financial innovation had shifted from the Italian city-states to the Low Countries, though it was still driven by the exigencies of costly and recurrent warfare and ambitions of monopolizing trade with the East. This spurt of European financial innovation had actually long preceded the Industrial Revolution, a complex but much better-studied chain of events. The financial and industrial revolutions then converge with the spread of joint-stock companies and proto-types of central banks in the latter half of the 19th century.

Ferguson explores distinctness of the European economic trajectory, beginning with how the majority of Florentine citizenry partook of financing the Republic's debt in the 14th century. In the 17th century, the United Provinces of the Netherlands combined the borrowing techniques of an Italian city-state "...with the scale of a nation-state". The Dutch were able to finance their wars by pitching Amsterdam "as the market for a whole range of new securities".[12] The 18th and 19th centuries are characterized by Anglo-French friction, but here Ferguson sees a yawning gap between protestant Britain (where public debt defaults became rarer and public debt itself increased manyfold; the powers of landed aristocracy became diminished and a professional civil service became more influential) — and Catholic France (where public offices were often sold to raise money; tax collection was farmed out and government bond issues lost credibility). Notably, the incremental spread of, and popular faith in, British government bonds allowed Whitehall to borrow overseas as well, much to the detriment of Napoleon's armies.

The forgoing passages might suggest that the economic balance of power between East and West had started shifting sometime around the 14th century. The downfall of the Mongol Empire and the Plague no doubt played a significant role in this process, but it should be noted that this is also a period when centuries-old Chinese inventions are absorbed in Europe, with military technology disseminated particularly quickly. By the 16th century, gunpowder applications were far more advanced in Europe than in China (the trebuchet arguably found its way to Europe much earlier). Paper and moveable printing were, of course, equally critical as they underpinned the spread literacy, bills of exchange, and paper money.

[12] *Ibid.*, p. 75.

Here, however, technological dissemination was much slower than was the case with weaponry: paper appeared in Moorish Spain in the 12th century but it was not until the 14th century that paper mills appeared in England.[13]

Navigation is another case in point as most experts agree that a compass of sorts had been in use by Chinese seafarers at least a century before Europe (i.e., 11th century). Similarly, the Song dynasty operated four-decker catapult-fire ships that were much bigger than anything in use in Europe at the time. But the advent of mechanical clockwork, the European version of the Islamic astrolabe, and the chronometer all came at the time when China had effectively been under self-imposed imperial maritime quarantine. European astronomers knew as early as the Middle Ages that the local time of an eclipse depended on the longitude, and in the 16th century, they pointed out the principle of determining longitude by comparing the local time with the reading of a clock that reliably kept the time of a known meridian. No such clock was then available, but in 1714, the British Parliament offered a prize of 20,000 pound sterling to anyone who could discover a method of finding the longitude within 30 miles during a sea voyage. The English inventor John Harrison was eventually awarded the prize for a chronometer tested in 1761–1762. His success heralded the practice of making timed observations of heavenly bodies at sea.[14]

Scheidel's observation about the level of monetization in Rome calls for a more detailed account of the technological as well as organizational development of mining in either region, not least because the European economy relied on metal coinage right up to first appearance of paper money there in the mid-17th century. A cursory comparison would suggest that, despite broadly similar excavation tools, Roman mining ventures were far more extensive, and went vertically deeper into the ground, than in early-imperial China. Many mines gradually became the property of the Roman state but — somewhat contrary to the overall Chinese pattern — cities and private individuals continued to own and operate *large-scale* mines. Even in its state-owned mines, Rome sometimes leased out operating contracts

---

[13] J. Needham, *Science and Civilisation in China*. 6 vols (Cambridge: Cambridge University Press, 1954–1988).

[14] E. G. R. Taylor, *The Haven-Finding Art: A History of Navigation from Odysseus to Captain Cook* (London: Hollis and Carter, 1956).

to individuals, small associations, or the larger *societates publicanorum* (or *publicani* in short) with slaves and wage laborers making up the actual workforce.[15]

Publicani consisted of *socii* (partners), who put up the capital and were governed by one or more *magistri*, who bought the contract. By the late Republic, they acted as bankers to the state and their messengers would transport mail for officials and important private individuals. In the late Republican era, there was even a market for unregistered shares (*partes*) in Roman *publicani*, which by now operated much like a cartel.[16] Can we trace the origins of early-modern Europe's distinctly large joint-stock trading enterprises right back to the legacy of Roman *publicani*? Whatever the answer, it would be difficult to find in imperial Chinese history a parallel to the role played by *publicani* in the Roman polity either in the mining sector or as tax-collectors for the state.

Conversely, it would be difficult to find in pre-modern Western history a parallel to the formative role played by salt, iron, and coinage state monopolies in early-imperial China. The intricate French Salt Gabelle comes of course to mind, but it did not coalesce until the early14th century. European early-modern monopolies otherwise seem more restricted in scope than the Chinese ones. In most cases, they were controlled by urban plutocracies with considerable political powers.

Notably, Chinese state monopolies seem much weaker after downfall of Yuan dynasty. Hence, when the British East India Company (EIC) — a *national* trading cartel for all intents and purposes — set up its base in Guangzhou in the late 18th century, it had to contend with a *local* cartel (the Cohong merchants). However, a mandarin was directly in charge of the Cohong (Hoppo), arbitrarily squeezing it for protection fees from time

---

[15] J. C. Edmondson, *Two Industries in Roman Lusitania: Mining and Garum Production* (Oxford, England: B. A. R, 1987); J. F. Healy, *Mining and Metallurgy in the Greek and Roman World* (London: Thames and Hudson, 1978).

[16] E. Badian, *Publicans and Sinners: Private Enterprise in the Service of the Roman Republic* (Ithaca, NY: Cornell University Press, 1972); J. R. Love, *Antiquity and Capitalism: Max Weber and the Sociological Foundations of Roman Civilization* (London: Routledge, 1991), pp. 175–189; U. Malmendier, "Roman Shares", in N. Goetzmann and K. Geer (eds.), *The Origins of Value: The Financial Innovations That Created Modern Capital Markets* (Oxford: Oxford University Press, 2005).

to time, whereas the EIC from its very outset was enshrined in civil law; it was free from managerial interference or arbitrary fiscal exaction by the Crown.

Unlike the EIC — or Roman cartels for that matter — merchants from the Italian city-states of the Middle Ages appear to have been able to reside and freely trade in China's hinterland. A better understanding of the Italian global trade thrust in that era, which eventually led to the discovery of the New World, might help scholars conceptualize the origins of modernity more clearly.

By the same token, the economic resurgence of China in the late 20th century could provide fresh tips to scholars in search of meaningful commonalities across Eurasia. As indicated above, economic historians generally debate whether a Great Divergence had emerged between East and West anytime before the 18th century. Few, though, question the enormity of Britain's Industrial Revolution. Rather, there is some disagreement here around the dynamics of technological catch-up in the rest of the world. The epistemological gap stretching between the periods covered by Walter Scheidel and James Lee's respective volumes could therefore be filled by reference to other new work covering not just the interceding but also the subsequent period.

In 1992, the demographer Akira Hayami coined the term "Industrious Revolution" to characterize the Japanese path to modernization up to that point in time. Hayami believed that Japan had started to modernize during the Tokugawa era due to a shift from subsistence cultivation of rice to a market-driven cultivation. The supply of rice grew as a result of the intensification of labor inputs by rural households, a concomitant reduction in leisure time and dwindling of draft animals not suited to paddy fields. In stark contrast to the British trajectory, which was characterized by "increase in the importance of capital [and] the development of large-scale mechanized production", Tokugawa Japan economized on capital while increasing labor hours through a newly-instated ethos of industriousness epitomized by Kinjiro Ninomiya.[17] The same ethos carried over into the Meiji and post-war eras, eventually underpinning Japan's industrial

[17]A. Hayami (1992). "The Industrious Revolution", *Look Japan*, 38(436): 8–10.

built-up. That build-up, according to Hayami, was initially driven by rural cottage industry rather than by large impersonal corporations.

Hayami's concept has since been enlarged by Kaoru Sugihara to encompass China's impressive economic performance over the last three decades. The "Industrious Revolution", according to Sugihara, is an alternative and "more dynamic" trail leading toward economic modernization than the one blazed by northeast Europe; it can be traced back to Meiji Japan at the earliest, but ensued in other East Asian countries after 1945 (Hong Kong, Korea, Taiwan, and as from the 1980s — China). The main impetus there was improvement in the productivity of the "peasant family economy" through the rapid universalization of primary education, and acceleration of female participation in the workforce. This, in turn, yielded a correction of the sex ratio in the population. By contrast, improvement in the quality of labor was allegedly gained in the West on the back of geographical factors (urbanization, colonization, and trade specialization).[18]

Sugihara's concept of a distinctly East Asian Industrious Revolution stretching into the 21st century, and epitomized by rural "cottage industry", may be critiqued on two fronts. To begin with, it seems that a highly-developed urban financial sector and the enshrinement of property rights cannot be overlooked in portraying Meiji Japan's tilt at industrialization. Indeed, perhaps under the influence of Gerschenkronian theory, most scholars have until recently attributed Japan's pre-war industrialization precisely to the fact that it rapidly turned into a "bank-centered" economy. Or in other words, the Japanese economy during the first half of the last century is often cast as the fief of powerful state-backed pyramidal groups (*zaibatsu*), each financing its manufacturing firms through preferential access to affiliate bank loans.[19]

But even if scholars reject this view as too urban-biased, Miwa and Ramseyer's new work has persuasively shown that industrial firms in pre-war Japan grew mainly through stock offering on the Tokyo and Osaka

[18]K. Sugihara (2007). "Labour-Intensive Industrialisation in Global History", *Australian Economic History Review*, 47(2): 121–154.

[19]C. Mosk, *Japanese Industrial History: Technology, Urbanization, and Economic Growth* (New York: M.E. Sharpe, 2001), pp. 31, 90–93, 199–201.

stock exchanges. Either way, then, it seems that the urban financial sector — not rural household credit lines — begot Japan's railways, petrochemical industry, and even its labor-intensive textile industry.[20]

A second criticism of Sugihara's concept was mounted more recently by Jan de Vries. He suggests that although the notion of an East-Asian Industrious Revolution is "not without a kernel of truth", it does overstate the divergence between East and West in the early-modern era. The roots of the Industrial and Industrious Revolutions can both be traced back to the spread of rural proto-industry in the 18th century across Eurasia. It is simply the case, according to Vries, that markets and specialization played a greater role in the West; European agricultural-labor productivity faced the same inherent downward pressures as in Asia but remained somewhat higher. In other words, countries like Britain or Sweden barely escaped Malthusian constraints before the 18th century not through rigid family planning but through commoditization and specialization of rural household produce, to the extent that married couples often worked at different locations to make ends meet.[21]

In view of these criticisms, it seems that the most compelling aspect of Sugihara's concept is his insistence that reliance on labor-intensive rural enterprise defines East Asia's post-war economic trajectory and that, as such, it does not necessitate *a priori* concession of property rights by the state. He cogently argues, furthermore, that Asian countries that had pursued a Western-style capital-intensive path to industrialization over the past half century (e.g., India) lagged behind, while those like Taiwan, which embraced labor-intensive industry and rural education reform early, grew fast. Sugihara similarly attributes the rise of China to the establishment of Rural and Township Enterprises (township and village enterprises (TVEs)) in the hinterland during the 1980s, thereby consigning the massive flow of

[20]Y. Miwa and J. M. Ramseyer (2002). "Banks and Economic Growth: Implications from Japanese History", *Journal of Law and Economics*, 45(2002): 127–164.

[21]See, e.g., J. de Vries, *The Industrious Revolution: Consumer Behaviour and the Household Economy, 1650 to the Present* (Cambridge: Cambridge University Press, 2008), p. 102: "[w]age labour, landless families and multiple employments had been a characteristic of most of Western Europe for a much longer period, and in this context individual labour rather than the collective labour of the family was the prevailing pattern".

direct foreign investment into Chinese coastal cities during the 1990s to a secondary role.[22]

Whither China?

The articulation of property rights, the status of women, and self-governing cities, as well as the dissemination of knowledge, all emerge as key components of the Great Divergence irrespective of which period one wishes to zoom in on. Yet, if Francis Fukuyama proposed just over a decade ago that the downfall of Communism would result in a Great Convergence across Eurasia with more and more countries opting for liberal democracy and civil society as a safeguard of a higher standard of living, 9/11 and the Chinese economic juggernaut have since interfered with the *End of History*.[23] In fact, several prominent scholars portray China's rising urban middle classes as politically apathetic, and point to sophisticated co-optation mechanisms of entrepreneurial talent by the party-state.[24]

Furthermore, after nearly two decades of breakaway industrial development in coastal provinces under Jiang Zemin, there are increasing signs that the current leadership might soon turn inward to raise flagging living standards in the rural hinterland. Thus, the TVE model highlighted by Sugihara might come to the fore again. But whether such a turnaround, if embarked on in the first place, might also be accompanied by a meaningful land reform empowering cash-strapped peasants to directly sell their plots or form interest groups after decades of collective ownership remains moot.

While economic historians await the announcement (or indefinite mothballing) of a new PRC rural land-reform, they can ruminate in the meantime on its possible implications for the Great Divergence debate. As

---

[22]K. Sugihara (2007). "Labour-Intensive Industrialisation in Global History", *Australian Economic History Review*, 47(2): 121–154.

[23]F. Fukuyama, *The End of History and the Last Man* (New York: Free Press, 1992).

[24]B. Krug and H. Hendrischke (eds.), *The Chinese Economy in the 21st Century: Enterprise and Business Behaviour* (Cheltenham, England: Edward Elgar, 2007); K. S. Tsai , *Capitalism without Democracy: The Private Sector in Contemporary China* (Ithaca, NY: Cornell University Press, 2007); D. S. G. Goodman (ed.), *The New Rich in China: Future Rulers, Present Lives* (London: Routledge, 2008); Y. Huang. *Capitalism with Chinese Characteristics: Entrepreneurship and the State* (Cambridge: Cambridge University Press, 2008).

for the "Great Divergence" itself — one can humorously hypothesize that even if it never existed at all, a divergence of some sort would have to be invented in order to revitalize the discipline of economic history. Already, it is clear that the debate surrounding this California-School neologism helped economic historians gain new audiences amid what is a fast-changing academic environment.

Chapter 2

How Unique Is Today's "China Model"

> It is the idea of parental and filial relation, which is so prominent in the classics, that introduces, not alone into the family, but into the structure of the government of China, its absolute and despotic element; and yet, at the same time, it introduces an important element of democracy. (T. R. Jernigan, 1904, *China's Business Methods and Policy*, London: Kelly & Walsh, p. 64).

With the United States losing its S&P "Triple-A" badge, the Eurozone teetering on the abyss, and India just not delivering the goods despite outrageously positive press, pundits weighing up the odds for a Chinese century have all had an interesting year in which to dabble in speculation. By way of corroborating evidence, even the leader of China's one-time great Eurasian benefactor, Dmitry Medvedev, weighed in; Medvedev was quoted in the party-state media back in June as acknowledging that Russia needed to emulate the Beijing's economic-reform formulae.[1]

Arguably, a "China Model" could never look better than at that surreal moment later in August when, not long after many had actually predicted the cybernetic overflow of the Arab spring onto China, the democratically elected prime minister of Britain, David Cameron, suggested that he would consider monitoring social media, just as the People's Republic of China (PRC) would.[2] If this were not enough, a long procession of luminaries from Joseph Stieglitz to Warren Buffett — along with Occupy Movement activists — all seemed to trash neoclassical orthodoxy, warning that the

[1] See, e.g., http://news.xinhuanet.com/world/2011-06/20/c_121557744.htm.

[2] Available at: http://www.nytimes.com/2011/06/05/opinion/05friedman.html?_r=1&hp; http://www.theatlantic.com/international/archive/2011/06/is-the-china-model-failing/240773/; http://www.nytimes.com/2011/08/12/world/europe/12iht-social12.html.

United States was fast becoming a "plutocracy" and that capitalism was "broken".[3]

Stephen M. Walt's essay, "The End of the American Era", has sounded perhaps the most succinct death knell for the sort of Western triumphalism that had emerged after the fall of the Berlin Wall, and which crystallized during the Asian financial crisis, persisting right up to the current global financial crisis: "[I]t is now clear that the US financial system was itself deeply corrupt and that much of its economic growth was an illusory bubble. Other states have reason to disregard Washington's advice and to pursue economic strategies of their own making".[4]

Unimpressed, other eminent voices have more recently joined the ranks of veteran Western sinoskeptics, raising not so much the familiar specter of corruption eating away at the bedrock of PRC economic performance — but pointing to a fast cooling property market with some disturbing subprime symptoms and a Japanese lost decade-like investment glut.[5] US officials, on their part, have by now become anxious to demonstrate that the Obama administration is not going to relinquish global primacy voluntarily. It is in this vein that Nicholas Burns proclaimed that, although the rise of China was the single most important issue facing the United States for the next 50 years, he was personally "betting on the American model, not the Chinese model".[6] All in all, therefore, this might be as good a time as any to try nailing down what the China Model, if ever there was one, actually means.

Drawing on two key sources (*In Search of China's Development Model* and *East Asian Multilateralism*),[7] this chapter is aimed at underscoring

---

[3]Available at: http://www.bloomberg.com/news/2011-03-22/buffett-says-u-s-moving-toward-pultocracy-themarker-reports.html; http://uk.finance.yahoo.com/news/Are-Free-Markets-A-Good-Thing-foolcouk-1531623804.html?x=0.

[4]Available at: http://nationalinterest.org/article/the-end-the-american-era-6037?page=show.

[5]Available at: http://www.nytimes.com/2011/12/19/opinion/krugman-will-china-break.html.

[6]Available at: http://www.theaustralian.com.au/national-affairs/opinion/us-bull-wants-help-in-the-china-shop/story-e6frgd0x-1226071257169.

[7]S. Philip Hsu, Y.-S. Wu, and S. Zhao (eds.), *In Search of China's Development Model: Beyond the Beijing Consensus* (London, New York: Routledge, 2011); K. E. Calder and F. Fukuyama (eds.), *East Asian Multilateralism* (Baltimore, MD: John Hopkins University Press, 2008).

the key features of China's economic reforms since 1978. Subsequently, the essay will examine how a more economically powerful China might alter the balance of power across East Asia. Before turning to the latest authoritative literature, one might recall that Western wonderment at the Chinese écoumène is nothing new; preoccupation with a putative, different China model long precedes 1978. Indeed, how the traditional Chinese polity worked, and to what extent it might have charted an alternative course to modernity, is a question with very serious implications.

Because pre- and early-modern history is more frequently invoked in the PRC academic discourse on China's global rise and its foreign policy than in English-language academic work on current affairs, it might be useful here to draw briefly on Thomas Jarnigan's observations, quoted above, for these observations bespeak an early 20th-century undercurrent, which subverted, in a sense, the more conventional Western view of the Chinese polity as unremittingly despotic. To some extent, such observations are also reminiscent of non-mainstream views of the contemporary Chinese economy, which cast informal institutions as important societal levelers. To be sure, Jarnigan was impressed with late-imperial institutions that have "atavistically" resurfaced at times: informally transferable land rights; guild auto-regulation; respect for local legal custom; public-service meritocracy; and — more recently — a Confucian nomenclature.[8]

As is well known, the downfall of the Qing dynasty in 1911 ushered in a decade of political fragmentation that entrenched China's portrayal as the "sick man of Asia". There was, thus, less room for wonderment at its traditional ways. Yet, interestingly enough, by 1924, even the acerbically Eurocentric *North-China Herald* could opine:[9]

> While China is still in a state of turmoil, it may seem absurd to write on any phase of alleged advancement when all that reaches us is news of internal unrest and military disorder. We have often pointed out in these columns that 99 percent of

[8]For a highly pertinent discussion of late-imperial Chinese political economy in European comparative perspective, see, e.g., R. B. Wong, *China Transformed: Historical Change and the Limits of European Experience* (Ithaca, NY: Cornell University Press, 1997). For the democratic potential in Chinese tradition, see, e.g., W. T. de Bary, *Asian Values and Human Rights: A Confucian Communitarian Perspective* (Cambridge, MA: Harvard University Press, 1998).

[9]"China's Industrial Future" (editorial), *North-China Herald*, December 19, 1924, p. 5.

> China's 400,000,000 care nothing for politics: their pressing care is rice, and the very wherewithal to live. China's history shows that this has ever been so, and despite the fact democratic principles worked out in habitual practice have held out inducements for the son of the lowliest labourer to rise to the highest position in the realm of politics, there has been an infinitesimal proportion of the people who have left agriculture and industry for politics. This is true to-day. For while we hear much more of internal politics than we used to, this whirr is made by an extremely small number of the people. But in a very real sense the masses are becoming gradually interested in industries, for there are already signs that China will some day become a great industrial power. Many Chinese, even at points far inland, whose forebears tilled the soil century after century, are now pulling cranks and levers instead of pushing their crude hoes or driving their ungainly buffaloes. Quality may not be, and is not, on a par with the foreign-made article, but it seems to be good enough for the vast interior markets. And as time goes on China will make many more commodities, and will not then have to buy elsewhere; the remark is applicable, if we take the long view, to practically anything from a cake of soap or a packet of needles to an aeroplane or a locomotive. . . . With reference to these figures it must be borne in mind that a considerable proportion of the goods mentioned are manufactured under foreign auspices, principally British and Japanese, and where this is not the case it should be noted that the article produced is at times of indeterminate quality. . . . Today, however, things are different. The Chinese are learning the way, are now turning out tolerably decent products that they find marketable in their own domestic markets and will continue year by year to increase their outputs to give them a surplus for export. . . . Instead of baulking industry, Chinese officials should be commercial missionaries. They should be patrons of industry. They surely must know that China possesses an unparalleled opportunity to forge ahead as an industrial country, and the Government must awaken to the fact that if industries are to be allowed to attain their full growth they will be able to yield much greater revenue then could be possibly obtained by crushing them by taxation at the outset.

The foregoing *Herald* piece makes very clear the stark differences between the 1920s and today's setting: Chinese central government is, for example, infinitely more powerful at present, with the best and brightest attracted to its bureaucracy; the population is more than three times bigger, of course, with city dwellers fast approaching almost half of the total for the first time in the country's history.[10] Yet, as *In Search of China's Development Model* demonstrates, a few of the *Herald* concerns surprisingly live on despite decades of central planning and Maoist upheaval: there are still

[10]Available at: http://www.bloomberg.com/news/2011-04-28/china-s-urban-population-climbs-to-49-7-of-total-nbs-says.html.

grave imbalances between the coastal and landlocked provinces; foreign-owned enterprise again plays a critical role in the economy; there is a perceived lack of innovation and pernicious intervention by the state; and the need to awaken consumerism further inland is again the stuff of headline news. In a sense, the second volume under review in this chapter, *East Asian Multilateralism*, makes for a convenient platform from which to revisit the *Herald*'s projection of almost a century ago: Is China, indeed, transforming into a great power?

Can a "China Model" Be Defined? Is It Exportable?

Published in 2012, *In Search of China's Development Model* (hereafter CM) is perhaps the most comprehensive attempt to date to juxtapose China's economic-reform trajectory against the broader sweep of the academic discourse on emerging economies. This edited volume brings together research papers by a few of the best-known economists, political scientists, and political-economy theorists pondering China's rise within American (and Taiwanese) academe: Scott Kennedy ("The Myth of the Beijing Consensus"); Suisheng Zhao ("The China Model of Development: Can It Replace the Western Model of Modernization"); Barry Naughton ("China's Distinctive System: Can It Be a Model for Others?"); Thomas G. Rawski ("Can China Sustain Rapid Growth Despite Flawed Institutions?"); Yi-Feng Tao ("Depoliticizing Central Banking"); Philip Hsu ("Power Competition"); Jacque deLisle ("Law and the China Development Model"); Chien-Wen Kou ("Elite Recruitment"); Bruce J. Dickson ("Crony Communism in China"); Hsin-Hsien Wang ("NGOs in Contemporary China"); and Szu-Chien Hsu ("Curbing Leading Cadres Power").

In the main, therefore, and quite like the second volume under review further below — CM showcases influential thought by US-trained scholars on current affairs; the volume does not seem, at any rate, to incorporate the views of scholars based in mainland China, or, for that matter, of those steeped in disciplines such as history. As explained in Hsu's introduction, the compelling need for a co-edited volume such as CM became clear as Latin America was moving away from the "Washington consensus", the latter being widely perceived as advocacy of unselective privatization and of small government. As well, it increasingly looked as if the PRC experience departed in meaningful ways from that of Japan and the little tigers in that foreign direct investment and low tariffs were actually promoted.

Naturally, CM straddles long-standing debates on whether the Chinese Communist Party (CCP) is adaptive enough to hold on to power over the next two decades, as discussed most notably in Minxin Pei and Dali Yang's influential monographs.[11] Hsu, like most other CM contributors, dwells on the dangers and precariousness of "crony capitalism" that is promoted by the party-state (CM, p. 12).

Kennedy's chapter is one of the best written, not least because it unflinchingly attempts the unfashionable: a defense of the currently much maligned Washington consensus. His is a qualified, well-argued, and factually based riposte to the alternative "Beijing consensus", as first articulated by Joshua Cooper Ramo.[12] For Kennedy, the way Ramo conceived of his revisionist "consensus" was wide off the mark (CM, pp. 32–33). He perceptively notes that two of the three economic-policy tenets identified by Ramo as key to China's success story have, in fact, been largely absent if not turned on their head: namely, technological innovation and equal distribution of income growth. There is otherwise little disagreement in the pertinent literature on the third tenet, which casts China as embracing globalization on its own terms, by rejecting the International Monetary Fund (IMF) counsel and avoiding loans therefrom.

Nonetheless, unfazed Beijing enthusiasts might take exception to Kennedy's interpretation of the country's success story as actually hinging on close adherence to Washington consensus precepts, such as strict fiscal discipline and maintaining a "competitive" exchange rate (CM, p. 34). To begin with, China's insistence on a managed, devalued currency in the face of Western demands has aroused accusations of mercantilist manipulation, so "competitive" would in this context appear a rather inappropriate label. Similarly, it does not make much sense to discount the degree to which Chinese fiscal discipline was relaxed so as to stimulate the economy in 2008,

---

[11] M. Pei, *China's Trapped Transition: The Limits of Developmental Autocracy* (Cambridge, MA: Harvard University Press, 2008); D. L. Yang, *Remaking the Chinese Leviathan: Market Transition and the Politics of Governance in China* (Stanford, CA: Stanford University Press, 2006).

[12] J. C. Ramo, *The Beijing Consensus* (London: London Foreign Policy Centre, 2004).

or the fact that China consistently defied counsel from most Western experts when it chose to keep key sectors of the economy, such as banking, aviation, and telecommunications, in government hands. Arguably, where China departed most notably from neoclassical orthodoxy was in its unapologetic prizing of big-government solutions over libertarian small-government ideals.

Apart from that, one might partly forgive Ramo's lack of academic precision when taking into account that the catchphrase he coined started filling a discursive vacuum; it brilliantly captured the zeitgeist and precociously set out the framework for later academic contributions, rather than articulating a comprehensive rebuttal of conventional wisdom in its own right. Kennedy is absolutely correct in observing that many PRC experts almost never cite an alternative Beijing consensus themselves, unless prompted by foreign colleagues (CM, p. 36). Yet, for all its inchoate and protean nature, the notion that a concrete China Model does exist may be gaining ground. It might be useful to recall in this context an observation Suisheng Zhao — one of CM's coeditors — has recently made elsewhere:[13]

> Chinese liberal intellectuals have always been sceptical of a unique China model and have argued that China's modernisation is not only aimed at building power and wealth but at introducing the values . . . of liberty, democracy and the rule of law. Despite this view, the China model as an intellectual symbol of national pride surged in popularity after the country successfully hosted the Olympic Games and the Western world was consumed by the financial crisis in 2008. For many Chinese people, their nation's recent success in weathering the financial crisis has passed judgment on the failure of the Western model and the rise of the China model, which features a strong authoritarian state to make use of capitalism and create wealth.

What does look like some Chinese academics' reluctance to discuss the Beijing consensus might, therefore, not only derive from the tenuousness of Ramo's conceptualization. Rather, other experiences of engaging with mainland scholars would suggest that an unwillingness to entertain openly the notion that the Chinese approach to economic policy might be globally relevant also stems from the political sensitivity of the issue or the fear

[13]S. Zhao (2011). "The China Model and the Authoritarian State", *East Asia Forum*, 3(2): 12–13.

it might uncork latent chauvinism. After all, the internal policy debate between Western-trained technocrats and their more doctrinaire colleagues in government concerning the next tranche of reform is far from over, and both sides seem to be wary of foreign connotations. There otherwise seems to be some reluctance in certain quarters of PRC academia to envision publicly the Chinese experience as a global model, so as not to arouse antagonism overseas, undermine China's putative uniqueness, or touch off uneasy analogies with the past.

Professor Zhao's CM chapter (CM, pp. 45–63) conveys skepticism about the existence of a distinct Chinese model on other grounds, too. Nonetheless, within the limitations of an authoritarian system, even Zhao calls attention to some of the party-state's successes. Cadre accountability, for example, seems much higher today than a decade ago; mid-level bureaucratic corruption is penalized quite systematically; regular decision-making fora and the concept of rule by law have almost completely supplanted informal Party gatherings as the ultimate source of authority.

Zhao's chapter further complements Kennedy's point of view when noting that the Chinese track record, while commanding awe overseas, still lacks enough moral appeal or "soft power" to resonate truly globally, simply because it has hitherto been "entirely guided by pragmatism" (CM, p. 59). Independent surveys have found that the Chinese are among "the most satisfied with their government", but the PRC "brand" is distrusted elsewhere (CM, p. 60). All in all, therefore, the Chinese experience offers important lessons, but its exportability is questionable, in Zhao's view.[14]

Naughton's chapter (CM, pp. 67–85) touches again on this important point, among many others. One of the best-known experts on the Chinese economy in the West, Naughton reminds CM readers that "there are no significant institutions that propagate the viewpoints of Beijing economists on a global stage". Later, Naughton seems at his best when momentarily shedding the neoclassical prism to decry "market fundamentalism".

[14]The extent to which China has successfully earned "soft power" overseas has become hotly debated in these pages. See P. G. Pickowicz, "China's Soft Power: The Case for a Critical and Multidimensional Approach", CRI 16(4): 439–455. *cf.* J. Kurlantzick, *Charm Offensive: How China's Soft Power Is Transforming the World* (New Haven, CT: Yale University Press, 2007).

In the "real world", he observes, extensive privatizations of the means of production — as the Washington consensus demands — could prove ineffective in countries where the regulatory environment is immature (CM, pp. 71–73).

Equally important, Naughton underscores the degree to which the organizational culture within China's ramshackle state-owned enterprises (SOEs) has been changing of late. Seen as deadweight on economic performance back in the 1990s, SOEs are today fewer in number, more profitable, and better-run. By the same token, Naughton corrects perceptions, also common in the 1990s, of foreign investment as being the all-important driver of the Chinese economy (CM, pp. 76–77). Rather, his account might suggest that the most striking characteristic of the reforms has been the Chinese government's mammoth investment in infrastructure. Such investment defied, for the most part, World Bank and IMF advice. In retrospect, China's success might owe much more than is commonly acknowledged to the government's intent on spinning off private savings and SOE retained profits into capital works, and its ability to constrain SOEs from siphoning profits off to corporate executives. China's paternalistic approach to capital works clearly contrasts with India's:

> China consistently builds infrastructure out ahead of demand; India only slowly builds infrastructure as bottle necks develops. Individual infrastructure investment decisions are probably made more efficiently in India, because they are based on such clear demand signals. But the Indian policy imposes large costs on other economic actors as they cope with bottlenecks and delays throughout the economy. Overall, the Chinese approach is better. (CM, p. 77).

Thomas Rawski, another prominent expert on the Chinese economy, goes a step further by hazarding by far the most optimistic prediction in this volume (CM, pp. 103–104):

> [F]lawed institutions are not likely to undermine China's medium-term economic prospects. . . . Although recent double-digit growth rates appear unsustainable, there is ample reason to expect China's economy to advance at rates that, while considerably below 10%, will ensure continued expansion of living standards for China's immense populace.

Where Rawski seems to depart substantively from Naughton's approach lies, perhaps, in his interpretation of the Chinese experience as one which, far from challenging neoclassical orthodoxy, actually debunks contending theories (CM, p. 87). That spectacular Chinese economic growth rates have been sustained over the last three decades in the face of "flawed institutions" provides, in Rawski's view, sufficient evidence that Douglass North had exaggerated the significance of secure property rights and a strong judiciary to Europe's economic take-off in the early-modern era.

This is a highly cogent argument that merits further study. In the interim, proponents of the new institutional economics, which North had inspired, might counter-argue that the bestowal of individual property rights and the professionalization of the PRC legal system were not missing at all from the Chinese experience. Quite to the contrary, these were gradually rolled out by trial and error along a trajectory that was quite often aligned with other ad hoc features of the reforms, such as the Town and Village Enterprises experiment with industrial collective ownership or fiscal federalism.[15] It might be, in this sense, a mistake to overlook the evolutionary significance of granting foreign investors security in the first instance, or conceive of property rights in neoclassical, binary terms. deLisle, for example, explains later in this volume that the granting of such rights to foreigners was an important means of kick-starting the Chinese economy in the special economic zones of the early 1980s (CM, p. 157).

Thus, it may be that the relatively smooth Chinese transition over three decades from a centrally planned economy to one where the private sector accounts for more than half of GDP could, in fact, mean that Western theorists and under-regulated financial markets have exaggerated the risk incentives and super-structural signals needed in order to propel would-be entrepreneurs into action and to reward corporate initiative. Medvedev's statement might also suggest that many Russians rue having bought into the dominant IMF discourse of the early 1990s, which placed a premium on such entrepreneurial incentives. Of course, this proposition cannot be fully borne out before the PRC demonstrates it can beget global greenfield-technology leaders through an alternative approach.

The third and fourth segments of the volume cover the political and socioeconomic dimensions of China's development path; they provide a

[15]Y. Qian, "How Reform Worked in China". CEPR Discussion Paper, No. 3447, 2002, pp. 1–62.

more detailed overview of some of the most recent concrete economic reform measures. They, therefore, make for a worthy supplement to the discussion even if brevity commands that they cannot be fully treated here. In a nutshell, these segments elaborate on themes ranging from the depoliti cization of the People's Bank of China, through to the standardization of Party decision-making mechanisms; advocacy of trade liberalization; the diffusion of limited land rights and sanctioning of greater residential mobility; the recruiting of overseas-trained experts into the party-state bureaucracy; the induction of wealthy entrepreneurs as Party members; and the intermittent campaigns against corruption.

Most authors in these segments seem to subscribe with Pei's portrayal of Chinese growth as one that is ultimately "trapped", or doomed to fail unless the party-state dramatically changes its colors. It might be befitting to adduce Bruce J. Dickson's observation (CM, p. 193) as a conclusive marker of the tenor that most chapters in these segments assume:[16]

> With the exception of a few high-profile corruption cases (such as Chen Liangyu and Beijing vice-mayor Liu Zhihua) the CCP has mostly targeted lower level officials for punishment.

An East Asian Challenge to US Hegemony?

As indicated above, the upshot of China's ability to side-step the global financial crisis so far has been, from an American perspective, a great disillusionment with Francis Fukuyama's famous "end of history" trope. Laments about the premature demise of American unipolarity have thus emerged willy-nilly even before actual American geo-strategic disengagement. It would, therefore, be only logical to return to Fukuyama for an up-to-date reading of Weltpolitik: Is the scholar most commonly associated with the euphoria shrouding the fall of the Berlin Wall still sticking to his guns?

In 2008, prominent political scientist Kent E. Calder apparently teamed up with Fukuyama to that end. The two coedited a volume entitled *East*

[16]Another notable corruption case at the high echelons of government was that of former Guangxi governor, Cheng Kejie, executed in 2000. See, e.g., B. Krug and H. Hendrischke, *The Economics of Corruption and Cronyism: An Institutional Approach*, ERIM Report Series in Research Management (Rotterdam: Rotterdam School of Management, December 2001).

Asian Multilateralism[17] (hereafter EAM) on the prospects of maintaining stability in East Asia, against the backdrop of China's rise and the perceived US decline. In one way or another, all EAM contributions aim at assessing whether greater East Asian strategic collaboration, predicated as it might be on an ascendant China, could eclipse the hub-and-spokes paradigm through which the United States has retained primacy in the region.

While certainly acknowledging new multilateral dynamics at play in the region, Calder, Fukuyama, and most of their collaborators strongly believe that US primacy will remain intact for a long time to come. Apart from Calder and Fukuyama's informative introduction (Calder, pp. 1–14) and conclusions (Calder, pp. 255–266), and their respective single-authored essays ("Critical Junctures and the Contours of Northeast Asian Regionalism", pp. 15–39; "The Security Architecture in Asia and American Foreign Policy", pp. 234–254), EAM consists of eight other contributions by some of the leading US-(and Korea-)based experts on East Asian security: Bruce Cumings ("The History and Practice of Unilateralism in East Asia"); David Hale ("The Outlook for Economic Integration in East Asia"); John Ravenhill ("The New Trade Bilateralism in East Asia"); Cheng-Chwee Kuik ("China's Evolving Multilateralism in Asia"); Daniel H. Rosen ("China and the Impracticality of Closed Regionalism"); Kazuhiko Togo ("Japan and the New Security Structures of Asian Multilateralism"); Sook-Jong Lee ("Korean Perspective on East Asian Regionalism"); and John Ikenberry ("A New Order in East Asia?").

EAM is replete with fascinating, often mutually reinforcing, insights, not all of which can be fully treated here. Calder and Fukuyama set the tone for much of the subsequent discussion when they note that while the United States emerged as the undisputed power in the Pacific after World War II, "with a monopoly on nuclear weapons and a powerful economy that comprised nearly half of global GDP", it did not use its position to resolve the small but potentially ruinous territorial disputes among Russia, Japan, Korea, and China over the southern Kurile Islands, Takeshima/Tokdo Islets, and Senkaku/Diaoyutai (Calder, p. 3).

Even if the United States were strategically to withdraw from Asia, the editors believe that these disputes would continue to divide the region for

[17] See https://jhupbooks.press.jhu.edu/content/east-asian-multilateralism.

many years to come. Concomitantly, the editors suggest that the United States intentionally sowed ambiguity in Japan's relations with North Asia through the San Francisco territorial settlement and that this ambiguity was only partly offset by the establishment of Asia-Pacific Economic Cooperation Forum (APEC) in 1989. Calder's single-authored contribution then shows just how beguiling and ideology-neutral international-relation considerations can be: for example, the United States and China, amid their intense strategic rivalry, could, in fact, join forces to stymy Japan when the latter ambitiously lobbied for the creation of an Asian Monetary Fund in 1997 (Calder, p. 30).

In much the same vein, Cumings suggests that the diplomatic architecture in Asia is under-institutionalized compared with the North Atlantic, the creation of the Association of Southeast Asian Nations (ASEAN) notwithstanding (on this point, see also Ikenberry, in Calder, p. 219). The short-lived Southeast Asia Treaty Organization (SEATO) was but a faint echo of NATO, and there is no regional equivalent to the European Union. Therefore, multilateral diplomacy across East Asia remained "something of a joke" (Calder, p. 41). Somewhat in accordance with the end-of-history trope, Cumings believes that the industrial powerhouses of Japan and South Korea will continue to communicate with one another mostly through the United States, and that the hub-and-spokes strategic edifice is in no immediate danger of disintegration. Cumings also seems skeptical whether the threat posed by North Korea's nuclear program could bring the countries of the region closer together, as the US deployment of US nuclear weapons in South Korea from 1958 to 1991 did not alter the pattern of communications much.

Notably, Cumings argues that US policy was not just about sowing ambiguity in Japan's interaction with its neighbors; in fact, the objective of President Kennedy's Pacific strategy was to economically re-embed Japan within East Asia as a means of jump-starting growth in South Korea and Taiwan. To that effect, the United States pressured South Korea to normalize relations with Japan in 1965 despite "strong resistance by Korean dissidents" (Calder, p. 46).

On the other hand, the famous rapport between President George W. Bush and Prime Minister Junichiro Koizumi worked to embolden "Japanese nationalists and reactionaries" much to the chagrin of the South

Korean and Chinese leadership (Calder, p. 53). This point is affirmed by Lee, when observing in his chapter that since 1965, "South Korea maintained a virtual alliance with Japan through a common ally, the United States, despite historical animosity and occasional rancour" (Calder, p. 199).

Cumings' skepticism is, to some extent, tempered by David Hale. The latter observes that despite the absence of bilateral free trade agreements, East Asia displays a "high level of trade integration" (Calder, p. 59); he believes this integration is likely to increase as Chinese overseas development aid looks set to match that of Japan within a decade, and to open up more markets as a result.[18] Equally important, the countries of the region hold together two-thirds of the US dollar reserves in the entire world, which ultimately means the United States could voluntarily opt to scale down its military presence in the region.

Ikenberry's chapter warns that — unless cautiously managed — China's 21st century rise might harbor the seeds of a destructive conflagration between an established and a rising power, a conflagration not dissimilar to the one that pitted post-Bismarckian Germany and Great Britain in World War I. However, Ikenberry hedges his bet by reminding EAM readers that other historic rivalries ended up quite differently (Calder, pp. 223–225): Britain quite voluntarily ceded global primacy to the United States after World War II; and despite many predictions to the contrary, Japan never ended up challenging US hegemony, not even at the height of its economic success in the 1980s. Neither did a reunified Germany under Helmut Kohl prove detrimental to EU cooperation in the 1990s, as first thought.

Fukuyama notes in a subsequent single-authored chapter that China's rise is not readily compatible with other historic settings of power transition. The United States and Britain, for example, shared "a common ethnicity, culture, and historical tradition" (Calder, p. 239). Unlike the United States or the former Union of Soviet Socialist Republics, China does not wish to "spread its own way of life around the world" (Calder, p. 240). Nevertheless, there is already some seminal academic work implicitly suggesting that Beijing might one day wish to reenact something like the Sinocentric or

[18]On Chinese overseas development aid, see also J. Reilly (2012). "A Norm-Taker or a Norm-Maker? Chinese Aid in Southeast Asia", *Journal of Contemporary China*, 21(73): 71–91.

Confucian premodern paradigm of relatively non-interventionist tributary relations, which are thought to have typified East Asian diplomacy in the early-modern era.[19] For the most part, such scenarios seem to run counter to Fukuyama's projections.

The modern PRC, one might add, is not yet meaningfully tied to a grand imperial narrative in the historic Western or Japanese sense of, for example, spreading Christianity; flirting with Buddhism and Pan-Asianism to fight off white-man domination; or championing free trade, democracy, and human rights. Hence, China as a developing nation still has the luxury of adapting its universal message in what are fluid circumstances.

Reflections

While it is quite easy to couch the US–China rivalry of the 21st century in terms of an established power (e.g., British Empire) coming to terms with a rising one (e.g., unified Germany), there is, of course, much more that is intellectually at stake. Pedants might quibble that, in fact, the rivalry is between an older power (China) that is awakening to a much younger and more vigorous power (the United States) that has become disoriented of late.

Both CM and EAM are exceedingly thought-provoking in that they suggest that any simplistic portrayals of a politically divided yet corruption-free and morally upright democracy (United States) vying for global primacy with an efficiently run but repressive and deeply corrupt party-state (China) may not be very useful. For all their stark differences, there are a few startling similarities between the two countries to which one might humorously point: they both seem to put a huge portion of their population behind bars, and look pretty comfortable with capital punishment and with sky-high Gini social inequality measures. Indeed, the suspicion with which Chinese inbound investment is viewed around the world might well ignite in the future something akin to the kind of visceral anti-Americanism one can find in Central America or the Middle East. In his recently-published tome, *On China* (Penguin, 2011), Kissinger characteristically

[19]D. C. Kang, *East Asia Before the West: Five Centuries of Trade and Tribute* (New York: Columbia University Press, 2010).

noted that (p. 520):

> The United States and China have been not so much nation-states as continental expressions of cultural identities. Both have historically been driven to visions of universality by their economic and political achievements and their peoples' irrepressible energy and self-confidence. Both Chinese and American governments have frequently assumed a seamless identity between their national policies and the general interests of mankind.

Those two cases of "self-confidence" might invite speculation about a future showdown, quite irrespective of whether China's political system decides along the way to open up in order to become more palatable to citizens of the world. Yet China's unparalleled size, the realities of nuclear proliferation, and the climate challenges of the present era make it difficult to argue that its ascent on the global stage would neatly follow in the footsteps of the catastrophic Japanese or German imperial projects. Similarly, the impressive degree of openness China has shown to foreign ownership over the last three decades, or the gusto with which CCP elites are enrolling their heirs into elite US universities, are not entirely consonant with the post-war Japanese miracle. To be sure, Hsu notes that "none of the returnees have been assigned to any leading post in the Party apparatus" because of loyalty concerns (CM, p. 20). Yet, it is instructive to recall that even such a Mao enthusiast as Chongqing party secretary Bo Xilai did not shy from sending his offspring to Harvard.[20]

So, will China try, at the very least, to leverage its economic might in a bid to divest the region of US military presence, thereby proclaiming a kind of East Asian Monroe Doctrine soon? One would be naive to assume that China's recent commissioning of an aircraft-carrier or its extensive space program is designed for purely altruistic purposes. It would be tempting, from the Chinese perspective, to pursue regional hegemony in the long term, as even Calder and Fukuyama might agree. But it could no doubt prove counterproductive if attempted prematurely. Domestic politicking can, in any country, hijack a judiciously developed foreign-policy agenda. In this context, one might add, Foreign Minister Yang Jiechi's recent outburst at "small countries" — perhaps more than any foreign containment

[20]Available at: http://online.wsj.com/article/SB100014240531119044917045765725527 93150470.html.

measure — tarnished the credibility of the PRC's "peaceful-rise" rhetoric, and reignited tension around the Spratly Islands.[21]

For non-specialists, proximate readings of the volumes under review in this chapter would provide an invaluably trenchant introduction to the ins and outs of China's rise. Specialists, too, will no doubt be grateful for these wonderfully rich and theoretically bold accounts, while noting perhaps how fast the terms of reference in the China debate are changing. CM might, moreover, serve as a convenient gateway to several other important phenomena that are critical to our understanding of contemporary Chinese society, but require a more specialized study: the revival of Confucianism and Party ambivalence there toward; the gradual divestment of the PLA from civilian life; the changing status of women in the workforce, as compared perhaps with Japan and Korea; the espousal of meritocracy as a form of democracy and positive discrimination in favor of ethnic minorities in lower echelons of the party-state; and the increasingly boisterous media, blogosphere, and alternative-film scene,[22] to name but few.

Back in 2008, EAM dubbed the Japanese economy as "currently larger than China's" (Calder, p. 237). That this is no longer the case, or that the Obama administration has since EAM's publication fairly dramatically ramped up its Pacific rhetoric, does not necessarily detract from the volume's enticing prose or its topicality, but it does show how fluid the present transition period has become. For example, Cumings' EAM piece provocatively notes that "external observers might think that China, Japan, and Korea are linked by a common written language using Chinese ideographs, but in fact the common language of the region is English" (Calder, p. 48). Cumings' description is still very much valid. But anyone

[21] Available at: http://online.wsj.com/article/SB10001424052748704483004575523710432896610.html?mod=googlenews_wsj.

[22] Following is a cursory list of a few pioneering studies addressing some of these important dimensions. K. Louie, *Critiques of Confucius in Contemporary China* (Hong Kong: Chinese University Press, 1980); J. Makeham, *Lost Soul: "Confucianism" in Contemporary Chinese Academic Discourse* (Cambridge, MA: Harvard University Press, 2008); N. Li (ed.), *Chinese Civil–Military Relations: The Transformation of the People's Liberation Army* (London: Routledge, 2007); L. Edwards, *Gender, Politics, and Democracy: Women's Suffrage in China* (Stanford, CA: Stanford University Press, 2008); X. Zang, *Elite Dualism and Leadership Selection in China* (London: Routledge, 2004); S. L. Shirk, *Changing Media, Changing China* (New York: Oxford University Press, 2011).

who has been to Chinese campuses might wonder how the next cohort of Korean university graduates, thousands of whom have studied in the PRC, might change the state of play once they assume the leadership of their country.

If one is tempted to find, in conclusion, where the two volumes might synergistically be pointing to — it would have to be South Korea. Economically (and culturally) close to China, and quite often at loggerheads with Japan — this is one US ally whose reform lessons of the 1980s–1990s are highly germane to the PRC ongoing nation-building project; it is also a US ally whose strategic conduct in the near future might signal epochal movement, or indeed little shift, in the Pacific rim as a whole.

Chapter 3

Beyond Lu Xun: A Critique of Chinese Exceptionality, Meritocracy, and Historicity as Conceived in Wang Hui's Thought

Introduction

During much of the past decade, Professor Wang Hui (b. 1959), a literary scholar from Tsinghua University, has been better known as one of China's most controversial public intellectuals. An expert on Lu Xun's (1881–1936) work by training, Wang was awarded PhD in literature from Nanjing University in 1988, and would immediately afterwards take part in the 1989 Tiananmen student movement. Following the repression of the movement, Wang was sent for "re-education" in Shaanxi, and it was there that the plight of China's disenfranchised peasants and migrant laborers captured the focus of his attention. A frequent and much-admired visitor to US academia, Wang nevertheless became one of the most vocal critics of American neo-liberal policy prescripts as applied to Chinese economic reform. An editor of the high-brow journal *Dushu*, Wang cemented his position as patron of China neo-Maoist Left until his ouster from the journal in 2007. Though named in 2008 as one of the world's top 100 most influential thinkers by *Foreign Policy*, his reputation as prolific writer and public speaker has since been marred by recurrent allegations of plagiarism.

That said, neo-Maoist views are arguably much less controversial today — as People's Republic of China (PRC) intellectuals begin to more freely envisage American decline — than they were a decade ago. Moreover, China's New Left as a whole is seen as much less of a political challenge to incumbent Party leadership following Bo Xilai's incarceration last year.

Therefore, this is perhaps the right time to coolly engage with the historicity of Wang's thought insofar as it informs neo-Maoist views.

Here, perhaps the most obvious bugbear of China's New Left are pro-Western ("liberal") intellectuals, who wish for smaller government and ultimately a dilution of the Communist Party's monopoly on power, if not calling openly for constitutional democracy. Chinese "liberals" are usually more statist in orientation than "neo-liberal" intellectuals, but they are clearly at odds with individuals like Wang Hui in their perception of state embeddedness in Chinese early-modern history.[1] Liberals are also less critical of US foreign policy, and would rarely describe the Kosovo war as "imperialistic", as Wang does in line with the official Party line (p. 63).

Put baldly, for "liberals" and "neo-liberals", the pre-modern Chinese state as embodied in the imperial bureaucracy was predatory and all-pervasive, and these qualities are seen as having atavistically configured Chinese modernity as a whole. In that sense, there are some similarities between Chinese "liberal" and "neo-liberal" views and those of Karl Wittfogel, who at the height of the Cold War, castigated the Chinese pre-modern polity as one of "Oriental despotism".

Neo-Maoists like Wang are perhaps iconoclastic in that, contrary to Wittfogel's conventional wisdom, they actually view the Chinese pre-modern and early-modern polity as one where state embeddedness was tenuous. Of course, Mao Zedong is acknowledged to have changed that pattern of governance in the 1950s, ensconcing state power deep in the remotest and most rural of regions. Yet, in the neo-Maoist narrative, Deng Xiaoping's reforms of the 1980s have been catastrophic precisely because they rolled back state buffers, leaving under-developed parts of the country to fend for themselves. Thus, in the neo-Maoist narrative, the gradual removal of the "Iron Rice Bowl" (*tie fanwan*) — namely, life-time job security with complementary housing and healthcare — reduced the quality of life in China, and left the most vulnerable constituents of society tramped upon.

[1]Prominent pro-Western Chinese liberal thinkers include, among others, Nobel prize laureate Liu Xiaobo, film-maker Su Xiaokang, economist Mao Yushi, jurist He Weifang, historians Qin Hui and Xu Jilin, dissidents Li Zehou, Wang Juntao, and Chen Ziming. Prominent Chinese "neo-liberals" include, among others, economists Zhang Weiying and Chen Zhiwu.

Neo-Maoist dismiss the achievements of the reform era over the last three decades as mostly fanfare. In the face of all the stellar growth generated, they complain that inequality, displacement, pollution, consumerism, and political apathy were tolerated by the authorities to an excessive degree. They also allege that rampant privatization and state-asset stripping occurred, even though observers of the Chinese Communist Party can hardly label it Thatcherite, what with its protection of select massive state-owned enterprises (SOEs), and in view of the fact that the scale of privatization in 1990s China fell well short of Yeltsin's Russia.

Wang's Major English-Language Exposé

What is perhaps surprising about Wang's academic trajectory is that, despite his early-acquired reputation in the West, so little of his work had actually been translated into English so far. Rebecca Karl has thus rendered a fabulous service not just to the China Studies community but to many lay audiences in compiling a translation of Wang's key articles; Karl enables us to cast our academic gaze right at the essence of Wang's thought without being swayed by the worldly controversies and gossip that surround him.

Titled *The End of Revolution*,[2] this compilation allows readers to grapple with Wang's complex thought ahead of the completion of translation of his four-volume *magnum opus The Rise of Modern Chinese Thought* (*Xiandai Zhongguo sixiang de xingqi*) into English. Indeed, almost all of the themes Wang touches on in the latter appear in more accessible form here.

Wang's translators would probably agree when he describes his own writing style as "difficult, dense, and long" (*The End of Revolution*, p. 105) but his intimate understanding of the latest trends in Western humanities is, nevertheless, formidable. He is one of few PRC intellectuals who are equally at ease with post-colonial theoretical constructs like the "subaltern" as with pre-modern Confucian cosmological tropes such as the "heavenly principle" (*tianli*). Indeed, as much as it is about contemporary China, *The End of Revolution* is replete with references to prominent Western New Left theoreticians well beyond the English-speaking world, e.g., Althusser (p. 14), Gramsci (p. 15), and Foucault (pp. 70, 165).

[2]See http://www.versobooks.com/books/955-the-end-of-the-revolution.

Yet, the degree to which Wang Hui actually builds on these Western theoreticians in his argumentation is open to debate, not least because they were all fairly Eurocentric whilst Wang insists on Chinese historic distinctness. Here, however, my main concern does not lie with critiquiting Wang's theoretical formulations but with the historic "narratives" — to borrow New Left jargon — that underlies his observations about contemporary China.

To illustrate my case, it is perhaps best to begin with the kind of history that is ascribed to the very recent and much discussed Global Financial Crisis (2008). In his introduction (p. xxvii), Wang appears to offer an explanation for the Global Financial Crisis that might go down well with Naomi Klein enthusiasts but is rather short on specifics:

> The current financial crisis has shown that crises arise precisely from shifts in the autonomies of societies, so that a crisis elsewhere can quickly become China's own crisis, and these crises cannot be overcome simply by reasserting old ideals of sovereignty . . .

One may well empathize with the *global* movement against "globalization" to which Wang pertains, yet scholars in the humanities might owe their readers a little more than Luddite sound-bites if they wish to be seriously heeded in public debate. The problem with Wang's observation here is not so much in its forgone conclusion but in the kind of alternative recent histories it brushes aside.

To begin with, one might immediately problematize Wang's facile observation by arguing that China was able to withstand the Global Financial Crisis better than the West precisely by re-asserting "the old ideals of sovereignty". In other words, China's insistence on a managed currency and an insular banking system served it well. Moreover, one might argue that China bucked the global neo-liberal thrust of the 1990s in important ways, and that the stimulus package it introduced in 2008 was comparatively much bigger than the one applied in panic-stricken "small-government" America.

In that sense, Wang might be easily mistaken here for writing about the 1997 Asian Financial Crisis where *Southeast* Asian countries did teeter on the brink of economic abyss due in part to the flight of hot money overseas, more open banking systems, and freely convertible currencies. Yet, in 1997 too, China was spared precisely because — one might argue — it refused to surrender to neo-liberal conventional wisdom. To be sure, later in the book, Wang does come to touch on the 1997 crisis specifically, yet, he inexplicably passes up the opportunity of offering any concrete lessons for China therefrom save for the rather abstruse dictum that (p. 90): "... external causes arise themselves from internal causes".

Wang is otherwise not entirely unaware of China's uniqueness in bucking the neo-liberal trend — he does laconically notes elsewhere in his introduction, for example, that land had not been privatized in China (p. xxxii). However, despite his good intentions, he fails to put this observation into a persuasive and coherent framework that might bear out his case for Chinese historic exceptionality.

Intellectual integrity (if not dialectic materialism) might require PRC leftists to show not just opprobrium against the ills of economic reform, but also to acknowledge that in many other ways, China was perhaps the single greatest "beneficiary of globalization" over the past three decades, as George Soros put it.[3] In the words of Zheng Yongnian — one of the most influential "China Model" theoreticians in the world today — the PRC's reform era of the last three decades embodies to a great extent the pre-modern Chinese tenet of always sticking to middle ground and avoiding either extreme (*zhongyong*). In the post-1979 setting, that tenet instructed avoidance of neo-liberal market fundamentalism even when that ideology was globally much more popular, hence China's ability to pre-empt state asset stripping as occurred in Yeltsin's Russia. At the same time, the centrally-planned economy was made to selectively and gradually give way to market forces, with social buffers like dual-track pricing applied throughout.[4] Public intellectuals like Wang, who also see themselves as social activists, do inevitably need to coherently address the contradictions

---

[3]C. Freeland, "Around the Word with George Soros". Available at: http://blogs.reuters.com/chrystia-freeland/2010/09/15/around-the-world-with-george-soros/.

Reluctance to acknowledge China as a beneficiary of globalization is also characteristic of prominent left-wing China watchers based in Western academe such as A. Dirlk, "Globalisation and National Development: The Perspective of the Chinese Revolution", *CR: The New Centennial Review*, 3.2(2003): 241–270; "The Idea of a 'Chinese Model': A Critical Discussion", *China Information*, 26.3(2012): 277–302.

[4]See Y. Zheng, *Zhongguo Moshi: Jingyan yu kunju* (Beijing: Yangzhi wenhua, 2011), pp. 133–152.

Zheng has underscored in order to make more common sense and be taken more seriously outside the humanities.

Yet, as readers are taken further back in time, Wang's case appears less and less concrete, and his sense of historic causality grows rather elusive. On p. 77, for example, he dubs modern Chinese thought as "anti-modern modernity" — this is no verbal jugglery on Wang's part but in fact a very complex trope. However, it is only toward the very end of the book that Wang's various trains of thought come together close enough to capturing his rendition of Chinese modernity more lucidly.

In the first instance, Wang tersely explains (p. 77) that Chinese modernity was born out of the struggle against Western colonial domination. When the colonial burden was finally removed, ironically, the worship of Western rationalism became even more entrenched among Chinese political and intellectual elites. But that description might qualify Chinese modernity as simply "anti-colonial Westernization".

Here, again, academic rigor might challenge Wang, the neo-Maoist, to make his case more compelling. In hindsight, did Maoist ideology, for example, not precipitate a Chinese backlash against the oppressive rationalism of Soviet-style Marxism? Or, at the very least, readers might expect Wang — as a Lu Xun expert — to discuss the great author's role in advancing the "worship" of rationalism in China.

It appears that all too often, Wang's prose eschews such concrete analyses in pursuit of navel-gazing. Perhaps, the best example for this penchant comes when Wang casually observes: "From an intellectual perspective, Chinese postmodernity and Chinese Enlightenment are in sharp opposition to one another, yet in reality, they both view modernity as a whole, and simply disagree with one another on the question of timeline" (p. 79).

Needless to say, this observation is devoid of any actual timelines, nor does it divulge protagonists' names for that matter. As well, with so much mention of "modernity" in Wang's *oeuvre*, readers can hardly be expected to take Wang's subsequent disclaimer at face value: "Seeking out a standard definition of modernity is not my interest" (p. 80).

Wang's fury at the residual worship of Western rationalism in China, and the Hegelian bias it speaks to, might still be justified for all we know. Inevitably, however, he appears to be tilting at early 20th-century windmills in the academic realm because so much of what he writes about concerns intellectual debates following the May Fourth Movement of 1919. Though not necessarily cited by Wang, a truly gigantic body of literature has already built up concerning that Movement and its over-rationalist bent.[5]

In critiquing the "over-rationalist" spirit of the May Fourth Movement, Wang seems to be smartly charting other historic paths to modernity or, in other words, socially mellower alternatives to nation-statehood in its early-modern Western iteration. Yet, readers cannot escape the feeling that the alternative on offer is not just elusive but that the rendition is awfully reminiscent of ideas they might have come across elsewhere. To be more precise, Wang's critique of Western nation-statehood as repressively thrust (or self-inflicted) upon Asia seems a throwback to Prasenjit Duara's *Rescuing History from the Nation* (University of Chicago Press, 1996).

Duara's treatment of the subject was, in turn, an impressively *detailed* riposte to Joseph Levenson's influential work in the field of Chinese history, whereby Levenson portrayed proponents of tradition in early 20th-century China like Liang Qichao or Zhang Binglin as un-selfconscious as compared with the pro-Western modernizers of the May Fourth Movement. Duara brilliantly drew parallels between Liang, Zhang, and the *conscious* if tentative pan-Asianism of Tagore and Gandhi in charting what might have been a softer Asian alternative to organizing the late-colonial world. He also underscored Marxism and Shi'ite fundamentalism as challenges to the modern nation-state bailiwick, and discussed at length the sub-ethnic and class strains than inherently subverted the cohesion of the nation state.

Following Duara (p. 57) and (more recently) some Chinese foreign-policy theoreticians, Wang seems to be pointing at other possibilities where perhaps the Chinese civilizational trope *Tianxia* ("All under Heaven") could be resurrected so as to relax the particularist strait jacket of the Westphalian world order.[6]

---

[5]For a useful overview of that literature, see e.g., R. Mitter, *A Bitter Revolution: China's Struggle with the Modern World* (Oxford, 2004), Chapters 1–4.

[6]A. Carlson (2011). "Moving Beyond Sovereignty? A Brief Consideration of Recent Changes in China's Approach to International Order and the Emergence of the *Tianxia* Concept", *Journal of Contemporary China*, 20.68: 89–102.

Notably, Lucian Pye had observed a long time ago that China was unique in being a civilization pretending to be a nation state. In that sense, Wang and Duara's ideas certainly tap into a rich vein. More recently, Chinese exceptionality was underscored along much the same lines by "China Model" exponents Martin Jacques and Zhang Weiwei. All of these thinkers predict that China's path to super-powerdom would be different to the one charted by the European powers and America. Because pre-modern China was a civilizational rather than an all-pervasive polity — Wang, Zhang, and Jacques' readers are led to believe that China would not be imperialistic on the world stage. Rather, it would settle for symbolic (read: tributary) recognition of its new leading status.

This may well turn out to be the case but in practicality, China is still sticking by the Westphalian protocol at least as ardently as the West. Note, for example, the pomp with which leaders from among the smallest and poorest countries of the world are traditionally regaled with when meeting dignitaries in Beijing. That pomp betokens an insistence on treating sovereign states as equal, quite in contrast to the pre-modern hierarchical *Tianxia* framework.

More to the point, Pye's civilizational argument understates Mao's achievement in unifying the country, spreading Mandarin as the official language, lifting up literacy, and coalescing national identity through a partly — imagined narrative of a New China (*Xinhua*). It is therefore surprising that a neo-Maoist like Wang should brush aside the mammoth nation-building project of the Mao era without explicitly discussing the nature of what went on at that time, and precisely how his softer civilizational framework can actually replace the well-tried paths of the West toward modern nationhood. Is the vague civilizational alternative to the nation-state straitjacket Wang seems to be advocating not an antidote to Mao's politicized China, which he himself often pines for in the book?

Readers are left to grope for the answer to this critical question themselves. All Wang is prepared to do is soliloquy rather enigmatically (pp. 116, 132):

> All universalisms are actually part of particular phenomenon, rather than simply existing within the dichotomy of particular universalisms.
>
> Is China then a nation-state or an Empire? We probably cannot answer this.

The inscrutability of these observations, one might conclude, is hardly remediated by Wang's sparse resort to footnotes, chronology, argumentative sequence, and other historians' formalisms. For example, his essay on "Modern Chinese Thought" starts on p. 105; after no fewer than 15 pages of rather scattershot and highly abstract introduction, readers are then advised that ". . . what I wish to speak more concretely about . . . is the question of empire and nation-state. . .". Regrettably, however, the "speaking" is rarely concretized thereafter beyond the kind of generalities exemplified above.

Mao and "New Democracy"

No self-respecting China scholar can duck the D-word, it would appear, without risking irrelevance. Somewhat like his fellow Tsinghua University academic, Yan Xuetong, Wang Hui alleges he supports "a more democratic future" for China (p. IX) but it is not clear what democracy he implies given his attacks on the depoliticization of Western societies.

Where exactly does he view himself on the spectrum between Scandinavian social-*democracy* and the one claimed by the Democratic People's Republic of Korea (DPRK)? Since he does not really disclose that with discernible conviction or precision, much of Wang's prose ultimately boils down to arm-chair dissent (see e.g., p. 93):

> I think that there are very few serious discussions of liberalism today, and virtually no serious studies of socialism. . .

Neo-Maoists are often vague about the "democratic" yet distinctly Chinese alternative to the tyranny of neo-liberalism and globalism: Wang is no exception. Rather, his prose is at its best when reviling what he calls "the old system" (p. 21), namely misguided and softy New-Deal-like social democracy. To him, one might conclude, Western social democracy is *ersatz*: a far cry from the promise "real" democracy as portrayed in utopian Maoist thought.

The underlying epistemological problem here to my mind is not semantics but the inability of both the New Left in the West and the neo-Maoist Left in China to accurately diagnose the Chinese model over three decades of breakneck economic reform. Have China's economic reforms been a case of mixed "neoliberalism and developmentalism" as Wang suggests (p. xvii)? And are not the two oxymoronic to begin with? Ironically, liberal foreign critics of China often accuse it of precisely the opposite — particularly as regards China's insistence on not privatizing key sectors of the economy.

Wang's somewhat mawkish passages about the Mao era (see e.g., pp. 48, 58–60) have credible and intelligible foundations that Westerners all too readily dismiss but these passages do not quite cohere into a robust critique of how Deng Xiaoping might have led the country any differently in the 1980s, given the dire straits he had faced. For example, Wang vehemently opposes rural land privatization and the lifting of curbs on rural migration (p. 13) but that was precisely the illiberal yet very successful path espoused by Deng.

Wang may well be correct in arguing that "neo-classical economics is itself a textbook case of globalized ideological hegemony" (pp. 15–16), but he does not give Deng, Jiang, and Hu enough credit for bucking the trend with their disregard for World Bank and IMF prescripts; their avoidance of foreign loans, and insistence on maintaining Chinese financial markets insular even as they remade other vital segments of the economy.

To be sure, most PRC citizens still respect Mao on balance in the face of debunking tomes newly published in the West. Chang and Holliday, in particular, have transgressed in telling the kind of story about China under Mao Westerners like to hear with their simplistic dichotomy of good and evil.[7]

But somehow, Wang Hui's rosy portrayal of the early 1950s in China, namely prior to the Great Leap Forward, does not sound reflexively critical either. This portrayal is quite oblivious to recent PRC research on how painful and destructive to social cohesions 1950s land collectivization proved (p. xxi)[8]:

> The agricultural class achieved a strong sense of political consciousness through the land revolution and a transition in the rural social order . . . It is difficult to imagine how traditional farmers and their village organisations would have

[7] J. Chang and J. Holliday, *Mao: The Unknown Story* (Random House, 2007).

[8] S. Hongjuan, *The Evolution of Land Rights and Social Reconstruction: A Study of Land Reform in Southern Jiangsu Province, 1949–1952*; Y. Zhang, *Diquan biandong yu shehui chonggou: Suzhou tudi gaige yanjiu, 1949–1952* (Shanghai Renmin Chubanshe, 2009).

> displayed such enthusiastic spirit of initiative if these social transformations had not occurred.

Not that we are necessarily persuaded by the revisionist literature in the West on China's pre-war economy, which implicitly suggests Mao's land reforms were redundant. Wang's pining for these land reforms is much less persuasive on the other hand: he ignores the fact that most farmers had been freeholders before the reform started; that the distribution of land before Mao was more equitable than in Latin America; and that Mao subsequently exploited peasants, and prevented them from moving into bigger cities so as to subsidize heavy industry and his atomic-bomb project. In that sense, the peasants who brought the CCP to power ended up ironically far behind city dwellers. As Wang himself acknowledges, it was only in 1978 that the rural–urban gap closed somewhat (pp. 23–24, 26).

Where Wang is much more persuasive is not so much in credibly laying out an alternative to China's so-called "neo-liberalism" but in arguing that the CCP has unabashedly become the party of big business under Jiang Zemin. In that sense, Wang sees little difference between China and Western democracies, where wealthy interest groups holds politician to ransom (pp. 6–8). Indeed, as indicated above, Wang is at his best when critiquing the dumbing-down effect of globalization and neo-liberal policy in a world consumed by consumerism and, one might add, Reality TV (pp. xxix–xxxi):

> . . . the dominant forms of the post-war political democracies were multi-party or two-party parliamentary systems, but under market conditions political parties are becoming less representative each day than they were in the early days of democracy . . . The interests and needs of the lower strata find no expression within the political sphere. As a result, they resort to a self-defensive anarchy.

Wang's real problems with globalization is not so much depoliticization but the growing suspicion with which humanities intellectuals are seen by Chinese society at large in our era as compared perhaps with the often-romanticized Yan'an of the late 1930s. One might think the end of the Cold War was mostly beneficial to the human condition, but in fact, Wang sees here (p. 7) ominous "de-theorization" of the ideological sphere in favor of practical focus on economic reform.

Is Wang's mission in his heart of hearts the restoration of class politics? If this is the case, then he is certainly not prepared to say so openly.

Instead, we find apologia for the excesses of the Cultural Revolution as (p. 11) "tragedy . . . [that] was a result of depoliticization". In other words, one might conclude that the original political intent behind the Cultural Revolution was *not* ignoble. Where historians all get it wrong, according to Wang, is in thinking the Revolution failed because it became overzealous; Wang tells us instead that the problem with the Cultural Revolution was that it ultimately turned *under*-zealous.

Matters of History, History Matters

Historians would have excused Wang's "difficult" prose more readily if only his discussion of modernity was supported by reference to more robust studies. However, footnotes are few and far between in *The End of Revolution*. Where footnotes do appear, they often point to Western sources by non-specialists even when the subject matter is China itself.

Relying on Frank's controversial work,[9] for example, Wang casually speculates: "[w]ithout *links* to the East, the Industrial Revolution probably could not have occurred" (p. XXXX). One could just as fancifully speculate: without India, America might not have been discovered.

Other than mystifying the already-mystified, what do observations such as these tell readers that they did not hear before? And if such transformative "links" existed, cannot they be concisely spelled out with sources and page numbers?

Wang further invokes Frank (p. 28) to curiously weigh into pre-modern Chinese economic history:

> On the subject of the currency system, and the use of silver and copper currency in various nations during the Five Dynasties, for instance, silver was the currency in use at the time (which is also to say that foreign trade was beginning to occur); by the Song Dynasty, the development of the copper currency system caused the original barter economy to develop into a money economy — which is to say a commodity or early market economy. . .

Here, the level of concrete detail is somewhat refreshing considering the degree of generality elsewhere. Yet, on perusing the details on offer,

[9]A. G. Frank, *ReOrient: Global Economy in the Asian Age* (University of California Press, 1998).

discerning economic historians might conclude that Wang is ambitiously (if not forcibly) hurtling towards too many expansive areas of exploration in the guise of an encyclopedist, where in fact, he is terribly ill-informed. It is not clear why the Five Dynasties era (CE 907–979) takes Wang's fancy in this book, but to suggest the currency at that time was mostly silver-based, and that foreign trade began to take off just then, betrays either ignorance of the most basic facts in Chinese monetary history or mistranslation.

Either way, when historic argumentation is so cavalier, those of us who work outside literature or cultural-studies departments might find it hard to take seriously Wang's call for reformation of the humanities and the razing of boundaries between softer and harder social sciences (p. 151):

> Modern humanities represent the disintegration of the human being instead of a reconstruction of the integrity of the human being, because, along with the separation of humanities from science, the concept of the human being is also separated from natural and socioeconomic activity.

By contrast, Wang's insistence on the historicity of Chinese meritocracy is more forgivable if only because the argument is advanced by so many other proponents of the "China Model" and "New Confucianism" across varied disciplines, who thereby highlight the remarkable longevity and uniqueness of China's imperial system (p. 135):

> In fact, there are now many studies showing that England's civil service system was inspired to a degree by China's civil service tradition.

Wang does not cite any of these "many studies"; but since the argument is heard more commonly nowadays in the public domain, and has become something of an urban legend, it seems the state of historic research here should be explained. The Northcote–Trevelyan Report on the British civil service (1853) is often described as a milestone after which political patronage in Britain declined in favor of life-long appointments of a political mandarins with broad liberal education. The Report is also credited with advancing the notion that recruitment of British civil servants should be based on a generalist examination system.[10]

[10]R. A. Chapman and J. R. Greenaway, *The Dynamics of Administrative Reform* (Taylor & Francis, 1980).

However, to my knowledge, there are no "many studies" based on *archival* material that might prove Northcote and Trevelyan had actually modeled their proposed examinations on China's generalist (read: Confucian) imperial examinations. It is more likely that they were inspired by the Prussian and French bureaucratic reforms at the time.[11] What is obvious from reading the op-ed pages of the London *Times* that year is that Northcote and Trevelyan were sarcastically attacked by their conservative critics as introducing backward "Chinese" ideas into Britain. Thus, the "Chinese" nature of the Northcote and Trevelyan Report had always been a straw horse in the 19th century — a horse which China's New Confucianism all-too-readily jump on, it seems, in the early 21st century.

Surely, the most authoritative *archival*-material-based study of China's imperial examination system published so far would be that of Professor Benjamin A. Elman of Princeton.[12] In general, Elman cast there many doubts about the extent to which that pre-modern examination system could be seen as meritocratic. But, in passing, he also showed that the system did entail at times severe sanctions against plagiarism or bribery of examiners as well as strict "avoidance" rules. Elman discusses (p. 201), in this context, Lu Xun's own grandfather, Zhou Fuqing (1838–1904), a Hanlin academician and fairly powerful local official in Shaoxing. Yet, even a powerful figure as Zhou could nevertheless be jailed in 1893 for allegedly attempting to bribe the local examination officer so that the latter would pass Zhou's relatives, thereby improving their chances of landing a position in the imperial bureaucracy. Incidentally, Lu Xun himself would later lampoon China's old examination-based "civil service" as irrational and fetid in his satire *Kong Yiji*, but that does not seem to impede here Wang Hui's celebration of Chinese meritocracy in times past.

Even where one might expect Wang to know better as a Lu Xun expert, and principally a scholar of early 20th-century China, problems of historicity arise (p. 103):

> The first generation of Chinese who sought constitutional democracy arose in the 1920s, and they carefully considered the class and racial conflicts of

---

[11] J. Greenaway (2004). "Celebrating Northcote/Trevelyan: Dispelling the Myths", *Public Policy and Administration*, 19.1(2004): 1–14.

[12] B. A. Elman, *A Cultural History of Civil Examination* (University of California Press, 2000).

> the West, making efforts to establish the broadest possible degree of political participation. . .

It is not entirely clear why Wang might wish to airbrush from the above passage China's much earlier experiment with democratically-elected provincial assemblies in 1905. Either way, even in the 1920s, Chinese liberals were more "statist" in their outlook than their Western interlocutors, as Edmund Fung, has shown. Fung also shows how even during the iconoclastic 1920s, a few leading Chinese intellectuals still wished to restore the tenets of Confucian statecraft, and how these intellectuals presaged in a sense today's semi-official Confucian revival in the PRC.[13] Fung's is a wonderfully detailed and concrete study of the period that might command respect not just from intellectual historians but from anyone with an appreciation of academic rigor.

Wang Hui's "neo-liberal" and other enemies within PRC academe are many. Their motivation may be ulterior. In the face of their condemnation, careful reading of *The End of Revolution* might actually reveal a fascinating social activist and dissenting public intellectual, who is quite unique in his breadth of knowledge and familiarity with Western theory. At the same time, if *The End of Revolution* is anything to go by — one might suspect that, beyond literary ruminations, Wang's thought elsewhere could well be similarly marred by dubious historicity and disdain for basic academic footwork.

[13]E. S. K. Fung, *The Intellectual Foundations of Chinese Modernity* (Cambridge University Press, 2010).

Chapter 4

Beyond *Tianxia*: Chinese Historicity, Meritocracy, and Exceptionality in Yan Xuetong's, Hu Angang's, and Pan Wei's Thought

> . . . Faced with the task of analysing developments or social practices in modern India, few if any social Indian scientists or social scientists of India would argue seriously with, say, the thirteenth-century logician Gangesa or with the grammarian and linguist philosopher Bartrihari (fifth to sixth centuries), or with the tenth or eleventh-century aesthetician Abhinavagupta. Sad though it is, one result of European colonial rule in South Asia is that the intellectual traditions once unbroken and alive in Sanskrit or Persian or Arabic are now only matters of historical research for most — perhaps all — modern social scientists in the region. They treat these traditions as truly dead, as history. (Dipesh Chakrabarty, 2000, pp. 5–6)

> American equality has always been sour, an attitude I would like to devour; My name is peace, this is my hour — can I get just a little bit of power?" (*Red Hot Chilli Peppers*, "The Power of Equality")

Introduction

Perhaps one of the lingering misconceptions about China in the West, at least among non-specialists, is that it is still a Stalinist country with an utterly mobilized press, and academics parroting uniform texts. Though run by the same Communist Party that came to power in 1949, China is far from intellectually monolithic nowadays, whereas its society has transformed into one of the world's most rivetingly inegalitarian. To be sure, the commercially-geared press is still tightly controlled by the state, and regularly censored, but it does nevertheless convey on occasion a very wide spectrum of thought on current affairs stretching from the highbrow liberal broadsheet *Nanfang zhoumo* ("Southern Weekend") to the nationalistic, steamy tabloid *Huanqiu shibao* ("Global Times").

Underway is, in short, an important yet at times quite introspective and mostly low-key debate across multiple tiers of PRC government and academe on where the country should be going next; a debate that — as this chapter might show — can on occasion evince streaks of genuine intellectual daring and exploration on the part of China's political, cultural, and business elites no less than it bespeaks pride in the country's achievements to date, or confidence in its future. And an even more daring debate might reveal itself, if one were to jump the "Great Firewall" (*fanqiang* 翻墙), i.e., breezily outsmart internet censorship, and tap into the issues preoccupying China's discontented urban youths (*fenqing* 憤青).

Yet, an errant netizen browsing through China Studies blogosphere and chat rooms in the English language might perhaps get the impression that the hosting of the Olympic Games in 2008, coupled as it was with the economic recession in the US, have buried Deng Xiaoping's "low profile" legacy; that they unleashed in Beijing sinister jingoism in every nook and cranny; that the Chinese Communist Party in its entirety is consumed by nothing but triumphalism, whereby it is arrogantly casting itself as the usher of a new "golden age", whilst its grip on power is paradoxically rendered as tenuous; or the impression that all Chinese intellectuals do from dawn to dusk is cogitate ways of restoring the country to its former glory.[1]

Quite often, omens of pseudo-historic resonance are injected into such condescending Western observations about contemporary China. That is to say, brilliant post-modernist tropes can be spun around, for example, train collisions with a view toward heightening the denial *as well as* hysteria which supposedly permeate the Party *at once*; toward

---

[1] Since 2009, Western commentaries in that vein have been fuelled in part by the publication of *Shengshi* (trans. *The Fat Years*, Doubleday, 2011), a searing satire about the nexus between political power, intellectual repression and greed on the Mainland by Hong Kong novelist Chan Koon-chung. Notably, Chan's novel has been officially banned on the Mainland, and feted as a masterpiece by Western China watchers. Yet, it is equally noteworthy that assertions of triumphalism by the PRC popular press have been harshly criticized by some PRC foreign-policy experts, whilst triumphalist policy overtones are attributed in part to a leadership malaise. See Y. Shi (2013). "Triumphalism' and Decision Making in China's Asia Policy", *Economic and Political Studies*, 1.1(2013): 107–119.

implying the imminent toppling of a corrupt regime by Jasmine-hued social unrest and the ultimate negation of its reform achievements, whilst at the same time projecting that very same regime as monstrously efficient; or indeed toward postulating some innate Western philosophical superiority over contemporary Asian thought (Ching, 2011).[2] Of course, politicians everywhere are very adept at spinning historic narratives out of context, and coining vacuous catch-phrases for worldly gains. To be perceived as a "Sinophile" is not media-genic in the West even if at heart one *is*.[3] But that so many of us in Western academe so readily replace the fundamental with the incidental in a bid to entrench a "new", though in fact rather conventionally hostile, interpretive approach to China's rise — one that is heavily subsidized by large quarters of our political establishment — might perhaps tell us more about Western detachment than bear out the fluid social conditions in today's developing world.

As the results of the recent 2011 Toronto Munk Debate on China have shown, Western audiences of both left- and right-wing leanings better receive assurances about the greatness of "our open society" from putative developing-world insiders likes of Fareed Zakaria than data that might question that very greatness.[4] Such lack of humility is in itself not very surprising. In the end, however, when academics voluntarily help our politicians peddle such humbug, they are in fact complicit in enhancing the same Asia-illiteracy that they themselves so often decry, and are funded to combat. This form of Western complacency is, as I have argued elsewhere, undermining the very thrust toward greater democracy and transparency around the world rather than promoting it.

To be sure, there is much that China can and will probably learn from the West and the academic freedoms we cherish. However, I suspect that the

---

[2]F. Ching, "What if the China Model Goes Bad", *The Diplomat* [online edition], August 2, 2011. Available at: http://thediplomat.com/2011/08/31/what-if-the-china-model-goes-bad/.

[3]For a revealing article on the Australian context of this hostility toward China, see, e.g., M. Sainsbury, "Kevin Rudd 'Breached Chinese Trust', says Geoff Raby", *The Australian* [online edition], June 4, 2012. Available at: http://www.theaustralian.com.au/national-affairs/foreign-affairs/rudd-breached-chinese-trust/story-fn59nm2j-1226382029072.

[4]The Munk Debates are a biannual series of debates on major policy issues held in Toronto, Canada since 2008. They are run by the Aurea Foundation, a charitable trust set up by mining magnate Peter Munk. Highlights of the 2011 Munk debate on China can be viewed at http://www.munkdebates.com/debates/china.

dwarfing of serious historical research in order to pursue news-cycle-driven, op-ed-style learning in publically-funded universities might not actually be one of those things that China will end up emulating in its race to lift academic standards at home. My argument here is that, those in academe who call themselves "historians" need to spend a decent amount of time getting the facts about Chinese history right, or better still — try to actually dig up something previously unknown about the past, before they scramble for the media with either theory-laden sound-bites or pocketbooks aimed at educating the public about the country's busiest tourist attractions and the supposedly narrow world view of its elites.

Much of Chinese history is of course in contention, and much we will probably never know for sure, or come to agree on — but the issues at stake do command respect rather than yet more "subversive" theory; the unsung pillars of research in the field do command decent funding: archival work, archaeological excavation, and fieldwork well beyond the hip art galleries of Shanghai and Beijing or the chatter of armchair revolutionaries. That is, at any rate, the principle whereby I propose to critique the "China Model" literature under review below. Albeit rare, factoids stating, for example, that all Chinese are vegetarian, or that all Chinese spoke the same language 1,000 years ago did exist in Western academic literature in previous decades.[5]

Though by now a not insubstantial body of work, "China Model" literature was until recently quite peripheral and rather ahistoric in nature. It was mainly penned by economists and other social scientist who aimed at generalizing how China's reforms worked since 1978.[6] Historians, to the extent they tried at all to find linkages between Deng Xiaoping's reforms and China's pre-1978 heritage, were rather minimalistic in their approach until recently. And since many economists reduced China's achievements to the inflow of foreign investment in pursuit of cheap labor and tax breaks, many historians also tended to view the Special Economic Zones set up by Deng as merely reincarnations of a well-tried formula whereby Westerners were

[5]For a detailed review of such slip-ups in Western academic literature on China, see e.g., C. Minglu and D. Goodman (2012). "The China Model: One Country, Six Authors", *Journal of Contemporary China*, 21.73(2012): 169–185.

[6]For a ground-breaking paper in this regard, see Y. Qian, "How Reform Worked in China", in D. Rodrik (ed.), *In Search of Prosperity: Analytic Narratives on Economic Growth* (Princeton University Press, 2003), pp. 297–333.

allowed to set up autonomous and bustling treaty ports along the China coast in the latter part of the 19th century. Those very same treaty ports had been, in turn, likened somewhat perfunctorily to the autonomous quarters of foreign merchants who had lived in China's ports from time immemorial, and whose descendants could on occasion even serve the imperial government, e.g., Pu Shougeng. In short, it was implicitly suggested that the reforms the PRC had embarked on in 1979 were not so boldly original or ingenious as might be otherwise assumed; that is at least until China started developing much greater ambition on the world stage.[7]

Perhaps ironically, because PRC academia in its advisory capacity is more tightly linked with government than in the West, one freely comes across in the PRC very sober academic accounts of the challenges the country is facing domestically and internationally, so long as the Party's monopoly on power is not challenged directly. One can even find there stimulating insight as to how the world might look like 20 years hence. In the following passages, I will address an important book in that vein by prominent Tsinghua University Professor, Yan Xuetong.[8] It is not a monograph in the strict sense of the word, but makes for a compilation of articles from various stages of the author's career.

Yan had already gained some exposure in the West, but this is his first major tilt at English-language readership. More interestingly, he spent several years in the US as a PhD student, yet returned home rather unimpressed with the American Dream. By commissioning the translation of Yan's works into English, editor and philosopher Daniel Bell has thus rendered a fabulous service not just to the China Studies community but to many lay audiences; for Bell enables us to cast our academic gaze

---

[7]Pu Shougeng (1205–1290) famously descended from a family of Arab merchants who had settled in Guangzhou. He served both the Song and Yuan dynasties as maritime trade commissioner. For influential discussions of the historic precursors to Deng's Special Economic Zones, see e.g., R. G. Wagner (1995). "The Role of the Foreign Community in the Chinese Public Sphere", *China Quarterly*, 142(1995): 423–444. *cf.* L. C. Reardon, *Crises Cycles in Chinese Foreign Economic Policy* (University of Washington Press, 2002). *cf.* J. K. Fairbank and Y.-T. Ssu, *Qing Administration* (Harvard University Press, 1939) for an iteration of the pre-war view of the treaty-ports as innocently grounded in ancient precedents of Sino-foreign accommodation.

[8]X. Yan, *Ancient Chinese Thought, Modern Chinese Power* (Princeton University Press, 2011).

right at the essence of Yan's thought without being swayed by the worldly controversies and gossip that surround him.[9]

Brevity precludes further discussion here of other leading Tsinghua academics like Qin Hui, who is usually associated with Western liberal thought, or like Wang Hui, who is considered one of the founding fathers of China's New (read: neo-Maoist) Left. Suffice it to mention that Qin's liberalism is, nevertheless, more grounded in the particularities of Chinese peasant history than in the Western historic experience, whilst Wang's radical leftism is better informed by intellectual currents outside China than was the case in Mao's era. Contrary to CCP orthodoxy, Qin sees exactions by nefarious local officialdom — *not* by gentry landlords — as the historic bane of China's peasantry, and for that reason Qin seems to pine at once for a Scandinavian-style welfare state *and* curbs on central authority, whilst Wang deplores the "withering away" of the state. Yan, Qin, and Wang are all from different disciplines: international relations, Chinese history, and literary criticism. Though equally interested in the historic long haul — and in contrast to Qin — Yan and Wang tend to see officialdom as part of the solution to China's problems rather than part of the problem (Qin, 2005, pp. 3–35).[10]

Yan is otherwise preoccupied with China's pre-imperial thinkers, particularly Xunzi (*cf.* BCE, 312–230). As discussed in the previous chapter, Wang is much more prone to cite Mao alongside late-imperial neo-Confucian philosophers; Wang self-consciously refers to himself as a humanities "intellectual", whilst Yan insists on scientific principles and rigorous predictive methodology in the social sciences; Wang constantly pitches to readers his involvement in the 1989 Tiananmen student movement as an important formative experience, while Yan — having been sent down to work in the countryside during the Cultural Revolution — might actually think of the 1989-student generation as misguided.[11]

---

[9]Before the publication of the book under review, Yan had already gained notoriety among US foreign-policy expert as an "assertive nationalist" and "neo-comm". M. Leonard, *What Does China Think?* (Harper Collins, 2008), p. 139.

[10]H. Qin (2005). "Tax and Fee Reform, Village Autonomy, and Central and Local Finance", *The Chinese Economy*, 38.6: 3–35.

[11]On China's New Confucianism, see e.g., J. Makeham, *Lost Soul: "Confucianism" in Contemporary Chinese Academic Discourse* (Harvard University Press, 2008); D. A. Bell, *China's New Confucianism: Politics and Everyday Life in a Changing Society* (Princeton University Press, 2010).

It thus quite naturally follows that Yan's and Wang's visions for the future of the country are different. Both, however, seem to aim in their unique ways at transcending the naked pragmatism, worship of GDP-growth figures, and materialism with which the reform era of the last three decades is associated. Both Yan and Wang are world-savvy, and reach out for audiences well beyond China; they are both concerned with the meaning of China's rise for the rest of the world. But whether either one of their visions can eventually win over non-Chinese audiences is quite another matter.

What Might China's Moral Claim to Global Leadership Look Like?

It has become widely accepted that China will soon overtake America's economic might, but that it will continue to lag behind America in terms of military might, technological innovation, and soft power for many decades to come. The CCP was smart enough to realize that vestigial Maoism can no longer entice "foreign friends", at least not in the developed world. Deng's pragmatism saved China from immiserization, yet pragmatism alone cannot inspire global audiences. So what might be the new global idiom through which Chinese power is communicated from here on? A new Confucian vocabulary has been conjured up at one point to complement the familiar rhetoric on the PRC's "Peaceful Rise" (*heping jueqi*) with hundreds of institutes bearing the Sage's name mushrooming all over the world. The Sage's large statue was even erected near Tiananmen Square, not far the Great Helmsman's mausoleum in 2012. Yet, quite apart from the healthy dose of scepticism with which this new Confucian garb was met with around the world, the fact that the statue was eventually removed after a few months speaks to the persistence of the PRC's socialist baggage and to the ambivalence within the Party itself about a resurrecting pre-1949 traditions.[12]

[12]On the removal of the statue, see A. Jacobs, "Confucius Statue Vanishes Near Tiananmen Square", *New York Times* [online edition], April 22, 2011. Available at: http://www.nytimes.com/2011/04/23/world/asia/23confucius.html?_r=0. On the persistence of the PRC Socialist baggage in "China Model" visionary literature, see W. A. Callahan (2012). "Sino-speak: Chinese Exceptionalism and the Politics of History", *Journal of Asian Studies*, 71.1(2012): 33–55.

In a recent influential monograph, David C. Kang suggested that China would not follow in the footsteps of Britain and the US. Rather, once powerful, China would try resurrecting the tributary system which arguably typified East Asia through much of the pre-modern era (Kang, 2010).[13] Yan, however, makes a point of rejecting this view. He does not believe the tributary system with China at its core can be applied to our highly inter-connected and inter-dependent world where foreign trade accounts for a much larger share of any country's economy, and where the equality between sovereign nations has become an entrenched norm (Yan, 2011, p. 204). If anything, in looking back at China's pre-imperial past, Yan intimates that he prefers to draw inspiration from Xunzi's normative realism than from Mencius, whose belief in the goodness of human nature is described as "unscientific" and incongruent with today's international relations.

Yan's interest in Xunzi's thought does not merely derive from a wish to tap into the New Confucian idiom sponsored by the CCP. His choice of exploring pre-imperial thought derives from a strong sense of affinity between the modern Westphalian world-order and the circumstance of the Warring States (Zhanguo) era, in which Xunzi had lived more than two millennia ago. The accuracy of Yan's interpretation of pre-imperial texts can and should be credibly critiqued by students of the period and philologists, but this particular constraint need not detain us as we are pursuing here the way China imagines its own history, no less than what went on.[14]

To his credit, Yan himself readily concedes that he is not so much interested in the historic veracity of the events discussed in pre-imperial classics like the Xunzi, but in the degree to which their rendition in the classics can be made relevant to the present age. Hardly a news-cyclist, Yan has at least devoted painstaking energy to the study of classical Chinese, and to the context in which Zhanguo classics were conceived.

He argues that (Yan, 2011, p. 202) "...the authenticity of these [Zhanguo-era classics] has no bearing on our ability to draw lessons from

[13]D. C. Kang, *East Asia Before the West: Five Centuries of Trade and Tribute* (Columbia University Press, 2010).

[14]Indeed, Yan's apparent indifference to the historicity of his case studies in criticized by one of his interlocutors in the book, Yang Qianru (Chapter 4).

them...", in the same way that very few Western international-relations experts would dare question the relevance of Thucydides' *History of the Peloponnesian War* on the grounds of historic veracity. Yan is nonetheless careful to note time and again that, unlike some of his colleagues in PRC academe, he is in fact *not* trying to assert an alternative Chinese theory of international relations using Zhanguo thought, but simply to enrich the dominant discourse of the discipline with insights from Chinese history.

Yan's reading of Xunzi leads him to believe that political power is more important than military might in the long run. For him, the USSR is a classic case in point, as it disintegrated precisely when reaching the height of its military capabilities (Yan, 2011, p. 80), hence the urgent need for China to find more persuasive organizing principles for its global rise. These principles must dispel what one of his interlocutors in the book, Xu Jun, dubs as the common view of China as "a state thirsty for power... [and] a serious threat to the stability of the international system" (Yan, 2011, p. 179). In response, Yan suggests that China should indeed exert every possible effort so as not to act like a new self-interested hegemon.

To my mind, another aspect of Yan's work is much more compelling and relevant to global audiences here: his intimate familiarity with the history of — and ceaseless attempts to draw lessons from — America's rise to global prominence in the early 20th century. Yan's mastery of Western international-relations theory, his close ties with his country's national-security establishment, as well as his belief in moral suasion and gradualism, make him sound at times like a Beijing variant of Joseph Nye figuratively attired in a Confucian scholars' robe. Like the Sage himself, Yan can and does innovate intellectually even while claiming to be merely transmitting. He is not unaware of this streak when stating for example (Yan, 2011, p. 141) that "... the essence of a strategy to attain hegemony is creativity, and imitation of strategies used in the past will never be successful".

Was Mao, the perceived nemesis of Chinese modernity, an innovator or transmitter in Yan's view? There are surprisingly few mentions of Mao in the book. At best, Yan briefly portrays Mao's United Front strategy against Japan as critical to PRC subsequent successes and legitimation (Yan, 2011, p. 143) whilst air-brushing, like so many other PRC commentators, the very definitive US contribution to the defeat of Axis powers. Mao's revolutionary and strategic genius apart, Yan seems to deftly skirt the very important but highly-charged issue of whether or not the Great Helmsman's era benefited on balance the Chinese economy, as compared with the living standards prevalent before the outbreak of the Pacific War (Bramall, 1993).[15] By contrast, Deng Xiaoping is mentioned more frequently as a policy innovator. However, Yan is equally explicit about the limitations of Deng's economic-reform bequest: "... it is only by constraining the worship of money formed by placing the priority on economic construction that the factors of comprehensive state power can be developed evenly ..." (Yan, 2011, pp. 141–142).

Quite unintentionally, and well beyond Zhanguo exegesis — Yan's book seems to undermine much of both the post-colonial *and* liberal paradigms that have proven so influential in Asian Studies during the 2000s. For in this book, Yan and his disciples own up to China's *new* circumstances of power; somewhat like US-trained New Qing Historians, Yan and his disciples cast aside the hoary obsession with themes of Asian individual and national victimhood under the European (post-)imperialist boot.[16] But far from accepting the Western boilerplate of modernity and power to which their country supposedly needs to adjust, Yan and his disciples engage — precisely like "modern social scientists" — with political concepts written in classical Chinese of more than 2,000 years ago so as to envision China's future. Whilst their interpretation of real or reconstructed historic events in the classics is open to dispute, theirs is an approach that greatly enriches Western academic literature on the PRC.

Unperturbed by Napoleon's famous warning about "sleeping China", most of us in Western humanities had missed the portents of Chinese super-powerdom in the first decade of this century. Indeed, even today, few Western commentators seem to believe that China would ever be capable or desirous of changing the rules of the international system. Uncannily, the dominant discourses in both post-colonial *and* liberal scholarly circles

---

[15]C. Bramall, *In Praise of Maoist Economic Planning: Living Standards and Economic Development in Sichuan since 1931* (Calrendon Press, 1993).

[16]On the scholars of "New Qing History" in the US, see e.g., J. Waley-Cohen, *Radical History Review*, 88(2004): 193–206.

worked in perfect harmony to play down China's rise, probably to the delight of those in the *Waijiaobu* who were in charge of executing Deng's "Low Profile" policy (Whiting, 1995).[17]

At least until 2008, far from theorizing the possible contours of future Chinese global leadership, much of the academic and popular literature on China in the West was caught up in speculation on the country's imminent disintegration. This tendency was, in a sense, a mirror image of Sovietology's failure to predict the demise of its own subject matter. That China's rise might one day force academics to re-evaluate the West's historic ascendancy or even transform the "rules of the game" was not much contemplated until recently, however plausible and tame the suggestion might be. At best, Western commentators would entertain the notion of the 21st century becoming an "Asian" one — a much more unthreatening, uncommittal and politically correct term than "the Chinese century". Even so, for many — acknowledging the "Asian century" would merely be about Asia's "future" catching up with Europe's "past" (Friedberg, 2000; Acharya, 2003/2004; Jacques, 2009).[18]

And yet, Yan and others insist on learning from Asia's past at least as much as they are preoccupied with Europe's. As if to challenge Chakrabarti's observation of India, PRC social scientists of the "China Model" streak insist on treating pre-modern Chinese thought precisely like traditions "unbroken and alive", from which one can intuit very practical startegems that might help China better govern itself, and set and an example to others. Along with its unconventional wisdom, Yan's book is refreshingly politically-incorrect and brutally candid on many different levels. In the face of post-war Western liberal sensitivities, he argues, for example, that nationalist sentiments are perfectly natural and legitimate in that they are akin to the desire for self-profit (Yan, 2011, p. 46). When explaining the appeal of political benevolence beyond military might, Yan can unfavorably

[17] A. S. Whiting (1995). "Chinese Nationalism and Foreign Policy after Deng", *China Quarterly*, 142(1995): 295–316.

[18] A. L. Friedberg (2000). "Will Europe's Past be Asia's Future?", *Survival*, 42.3(2000): 147–160; A. Acharya (2003–2004). "Will Asia's Future be Its Past?", *International Security*, 28.3(2003/2004): 149–164; M. Jacques, *When China Rules The World: The End of the Western World and the Birth of a New Global Order* (Penguin, 2009).

compare the Myanmar junta — until recently, a PRC ally — with the Pope, or later divulge in a revealing interview with Lu Xin that he ended up in the field of international relations not because of a deeply-felt passion but simply because this was the discipline assigned to him by government selectors as a graduate student (Yan, 2011, Appendix 2). Neither does Yan seem particularly taken — like so many in the neo-Maoist Left — with the argument that dispossession is the primary cause of Palestinian terrorism (Yan, 2011, p. 242).

On occasion, Yan hardly comes across as the triumphalist, doctrinaire "neo-communist" he is often portrayed like in the West. In fact, he would rather see his field of international relations becoming more rigorously predictive and less ideology-ridden than is the case at present. Yan repeatedly calls for a tad less *theory* in the field, because *theory* is often "... removed from reality", and thus better suits "unscientific" disciplines like philosophy (Yan, 2011, p. 244). Far from celebrating the unfolding of a Chinese golden age, Yan similarly predicts that it would take at least two more decades before Chinese universities can pass muster internationally; this is not a problem of funding or infrastructure, he avers, but the fact that "... we lack first-rate professors" (Yan, 2011, p. 237).

Replacing Deng's "Low-Profile" with What?

If Yan's arguments are to be taken seriously (as they should), then Western audiences might well conclude that China is gradually ditching Deng's policy of maintaining a low profile on the world stage, and might soon seek to more assertively challenge America's global pre-eminence. But the challenge that China will pose will not primarily be of a military nature, at least not initially. Rather, the PRC might initially dwell not just on its own recent history, but perhaps also on pre-imperial political theorists and on imperial statecraft in devising a comprehensive alternative to US unipolarity and the so-called "Washington Consensus". Yan suggests that in order to rally global support for a Chinese alternative to US hegemony, that alternative will need to be credibly based on the lofty principle of *wangdao*, commonly translated as "universal kingship" or "humane authority", and often contrasted with *badao* or hegemonic bullying (Yan, 2011, pp. 50–51).

One can certainly spend a lifetime discussing the complex Zhanguo setting in which this principle had been conceived; the reliability of the classics in describing that setting or the hermeneutics of later generations. Yan's concern for scientific truisms notwithstanding, the tenor of the book might suggest that what he is ultimately preoccupied with is *not* necessarily if and how *wangdao* was applied over the course of Chinese imperial history, but its potential as binding imagery for China's tilt at global hegemony. As already indicated, he is re-imagining *wangdao* as a visionary of Chinese modern power, not analyzing *wangdao* as a historian.

Baldly put, Yan believes that if China governs *itself* humanely, equitably, and in an environmentally-friendly manner, it will set an example to others, and pull countries into its orbit in the face of current US superiority in per-capita income, military deployment, and soft power. Arguably, China's one-party system has shown it can keep a lid on environmental crises, or effectively promote green energy in a top-down manner. China — Western critics might add — has already demonstrated that it can effectively rein in mighty multi-nationals like Google, but has not demonstrated it can nurture new technologically-revolutionary Googles of its own.

Neither has China demonstrated an ability to tackle the country's growing income disparity through progressive taxation or welfare reform. To be sure, contemporary China's New Confucians (not to be confused with late-imperial neo-Confucians) often invoke Mencius's "well-fields" (*jingtian*) ideal as one that has historically embedded egalitarianism within the agrarian Chinese mindset, and thus as a factor that helps explain the longevity of China's imperial order. It is believed that this Mencian ideal should continue to inspire today's reformers. On the other hand, most historians doubt the extent to which Mencius' ideal of equal land distribution and rural community harmony was ever applied over the course of Chinese pre-modern history, arguing that the Chinese imperial polity was essentially elitist despite occasional millenarian disruption. If anything, equal distribution of land by the state was the exception rather than the rule across pre-modern East Asia. Ironically, it was the seminomadic Tuoba rulers of the Northern Wei dynasty who most famously enacted an "equal fields" (*juntian*) policy in Northwest China rather than Han rulers in the South. Even so, in pursuing this policy, the Tuoba rulers were mainly concerned with resettling depopulated areas, not with creating an equal society as such (Lewis, 2009, pp. 133–140; Holcombe, 2011, p. 67; Woodside, 2009, pp. 56–76).[19]

As alluded to in the previous chapter, another *leitmotif* in New Confucian thought on China's future — inspired in equal measure by the modern Singaporean experience *and* the fabled imperial civil-service entry examinations (*keju*) — is the notion that deliberative meritocracy and state paternalism can replace Western-style liberal democracy because of their deeper historic roots in Chinese society. Meritocracy is seen, in that sense, as charting the possibilities of distinct Chinese modernity in the future just as, for some historians, the *keju* system went in fact so far as far as inspiring the formation of a disinterested British civil service in the 19th century.[20]

Nevertheless, in comparative terms, Singaporean officialdom remains much better paid and less corrupt, and the city-state's comprehensive public housing scheme much more progressive than the PRC's (Ortmann, 2012).[21] Proponents of meritocracy as substitute for Western-style democracy may otherwise be informed by popular and academic work which tends to overstate the degree of ideological cohesion, strategic foresight, and disinterested professionalism that used to exist within the imperial bureaucracy before 1912. The fact that holding office in pre-modern China had been popularly viewed as a well-trodden path to riches is important in this context. Also important is the fact that, in the absence of professional immunity, strategically sound advice might cost an official his life if proven

---

[19]M. E. Lewis, *China Between Empires: The Northern and Southern Dynasties* (Harvard University Press, 2009), pp. 133–140; C. Holcombe, *A History of East Asia: From the Origins of Civilization to the Twenty-First Century* (Cambridge University Press, 2011), p. 67; A. Woodside, *Lost Modernities: China, Vienam, Korea and the Hazards of World History* (Harvard University Press, 2009), pp. 56–76.

[20]Alexander Woodside's (2009) book remains the most eloquent in pursuing the modern qualities inherent in the *keju* system. That the *keju* system inspired the formation of the British was controversially suggested by Arnold J. Toynbee. See also R. K. Schoppa, "The Political Creativity of Late Imperial China", in B. Womack (ed.), *China's Rise in Historical Perspective* (Rowman & Littlefield, 2010), pp. 203–226. For a more critical review, see M. Elliott, "The Real China model", *International Herald* tribune [online edition], November 13, 2012. Available at: http://www.nytimes.com/2012/11/14/opinion/the-real-china-model.html?_r=0.

[21]S. Ortmann (2012). "The 'Beijing Consensus' and the 'Singapore Model': Unmasking the Myth of an Alternative Authoritarian State-Capitalist Model", *Journal of Chinese Economic and Business Studies*, 10.4(2012): 337–359.

too disruptive in the short-run because the opposing bureaucratic faction would often have the emperor's ear. By the 16th century, different citations from the same classics could often conceal starkly divergent world views within the bureaucracy even though "factionalism" as such was nominally forbidden.[22]

Yan takes this historically-framed discussion on meritocracy a big step further as he calls for China to embrace what appears to be an Australian-style skilled-migration program, and entice the world's best and brightest to live in the country. In that sense, he envisions a future China that will compete with the increasingly multicultural societies of developed Western countries on their own turf (Yan, 2011, p. 104), dwelling as he does on Zhanguo luminaries who moved from one state to another in pursuit of a benevolent ruler. Remarkably, Yan does not insist his future immigrants be stellar entrepreneurs or scientists only — he would also like to see modern-day "Pu Shougengs" recruited by the party-state as officials. Similarly, Yan is at pains not to project a future China as a hotbed of Han ethno-nationalism. Rather, he implicitly casts future China as a kind of secular, hyper-modern drawcard that would presumably counter religious fundamentalism of all strands the world over. He is, furthermore, convinced that China's internal logic as well as the wishes of the international community would not let the country follow in the footsteps of early-Showa Japan or turn into another version of Bush's America.

China's universalist, hyper-modern message to the world will be buttressed, according to Yan, by nurturing "strategic reliability" in the eyes of its neighbors. More specifically, and in the face of tensions currently simmering over the South China Sea and the Diaoyutai/Senkaku islets — Yan seems to be hinting here at very selective use of force or perhaps even territorial compromises, particularly vis-à-vis ASEAN member states. Notwithstanding negative perceptions of China's role in scuppering the 2009 UN Climate Change Conference in Copenhagen, Yan insists that Chinese

[22]On the benefits and risks of holding office, see Ho Ping-ti's classic, *The Ladder of Success in Imperial China* (1964). On bureaucratic factionalism in imperial China, see H. Dunstan, *Conflicting Counsels to Confuse the Age: A Documentary Study of Political Economy in Qing China, 1644–1840* (University of Michigan Press, 1996); A. D. Levine, *Divided by a Common Language: Factional Conflict in late Northern Song China* (University of Hawai'i Press, 2008).

"strategic reliability" would also entail China's make-over into the world's leading developer of greenfield environmental technology. On the environmental score, Yan seems to be echoing Hu Angang, a prominent Tsinghua economist, who is also loosely affiliated with the "China Model" school but whose work largely eschews longer-haul historic analyses (Hu, 2011).[23]

Quite apart from tensions within ASEAN concerning China's intentions, what might make Yan's advocacy of China's "strategic reliability" a little less convincing in Western ears is his depiction of China's aid to Africa as one that has historically been disinterested. Unlike the US, Yan argues, China does not make aid conditional on having a say in African countries' internal affairs or on their UN voting patterns. The only requisite is endorsement of the "one China" principle. Whilst Zimbabwe's Robert Mugabe and Sudan's Omar al-Bashir might enthusiastically endorse Yan's view, it is hardly the case that their endorsement would contribute much to the build-up of Chinese soft power elsewhere.

On the domestic front, as indicated above, Yan envisions a China that would exercise moral suasion through an exemplary distribution of wealth. Egalitarianism will eventually pave its way to global leadership. As Emilian Kavalski, aptly put it, this Chinese message to the world is one of "Do as I do" rather than the perceived Western imperative of "Do as I say" (Kavalski, 2009, pp. 1–18).[24] Cited above, Anthony Kiedis' powerful lyrics are perhaps a reminder of both the rage that social inequalities can generate *and* the cynicism with which politicians tap into precisely that rage without actually meaning to change much. Certainly, if China tackles inequality over the next decade as successfully as it tackled other challenges over the previous decades, it might win new admirers perhaps even in America.

For the time being, however, China's increasingly skewed income distribution means that — in the eyes of citizens of the world — it is an effective economic powerhouse but not a particularly desirable place to live in. Everyone seems to be calling for mitigating measures there, but other than rhetoric nothing much has been achieved yet. In that sense, Yan here seems to be merely chiming in with Hu Jintao's agit-prop call for a

---

[23]A. Hu, *China in 2020: A New Type of Superpower* (The Brookings Institute, 2011).

[24]E. Kavalski, "'Do as I do': the Global Politics of China's Regionalisation", in *Idem* (ed.), *China and the Global Politics of Regionalisation* (Ashgate, 2009), pp. 1–18.

"harmonious society" (*hexie shehui*). But, to his credit, Yan is also well aware that individual well-being in our modern age means much more than nutrition. Whilst prioritizing collective economic rights like employment over individual freedoms, he knows that the recipe for the longevity of China's imperial order — namely to keep peasants with "Full Bellies, Empty Minds" (*shifu xuxin*) — might no longer satisfy China's new urbanites (Yan, 2011, pp. 36, 102–103).[25]

Fu bu guo sandai: Taking the Debate on "Chinese Democracy" Further

Readers who are not experts in Confucian hermeneutics might find Yan's book ultimately posing at least as many questions about China's future as it aims to answer. It may be that Yan had to choose his words more carefully given his prominent status within the establishment, or that his penchant for brutal candor (for example, in explaining why he ended up in an International Relations department) is not all-encompassing. In order to get a better sense of Yan's vision, it is therefore necessary to reach for a much less known yet equally fascinating compilation of essays (trans. "The Strategy behind China's Rise") that he co-authored with fellow Tsinghua academic Sun Xuefeng back in 2005, a year in which China's "low profile" policy was still in effect (Yan and Sun, 2005).[26]

Sun's view here (Yan and Sun, 2005, Chapter 2), which seems to have been endorsed by Yan, was that rising powers can be more easily tempted to enter a limited nuclear confrontation than the global hegemon, which typically prefers the status quo. Yet, Sun argued that the Cold War experience showed such potential nuclear threats did not boil over or change the overall outcome, and so he was sceptical that China would follow a path where the USSR failed. But, like Kissinger, Sun did not discount the possibility of conventional war breaking out as a result of China's rise and Sino-American mutual suspicion (Kissinger, 2011).[27]

[25]On "Full Bellies, Empty Minds" in Chinese pre-modern statecraft, see Y. Pines, *Envisioning Eternal Empire: Chinese Political Thought of the Warring States Era* (University of Hawai'i Press, 2009), pp. 198–219.
[26]X. Yan and X. Sun, *Zhongguo jueqi ji qi zhanlue* (Peking University Press, 2005).
[27]H. Kissinger, *On China* (Penguin, 2011).

More importantly, Sun then argued that the common Western perception of democratic countries as less likely to go to war with one another ("democratic lineage theory") was irredeemably naïve. Notably, Sun pointed to the three Anglo-Dutch wars, fought over hegemony of global maritime trade during the latter part of the 17th century, as a classic counter-example. England had been at the time a nascent parliamentary democracy, and the Netherlands was a progressive Republic but neither showed "liberal trust" in its neighbor, and mutual draconization was rampant. As its power declined in the early 20th century, the British empire did not go into war with an ascendant US: this was *not* because the countries shared cultural baggage, but because containing the Kaiser was considered a more achievable goal. By 1900, America's GDP was nearly double than that of Britain, but Germany's GDP had just edged above Britain's and so the temptation to check the advancement of that Middle-European Power were therefore more compelling.

In a subsequent chapter penned by Yan himself, there are broader hints of his views than is the case in his English-language published work. For example, in order to rationalize Chinese popular resentment of America, Yan enumerates four critical factors at play (p. 220):

1. The US has been trying to check China's advancement in an under-hand manner, including through the perceived sabotage of Beijing's Olympic bid in 2000.
2. The US violated what may have been tacit agreements between Mao and Nixon by continuing to sell weapons to Taiwan.
3. NATO's bombardment of the Chinese embassy in Belgrad back in 1999 was intentional.
4. US foreign policy is tainted by double standards; it protects vulnerable players in the international system only when this might further its own interests, e.g., in Serbia but not in East Timor.

In *Ancient Chinese Thought*, Yan aims to some degree to steer clear of such controversial assertions. But he nevertheless re-affirms that in order to take the lead globally, China would have to exercise "reversed double standards" particularly toward the developing world. He recommends that China commit to more onerous obligations than it asks of other nations insofar as resolving border disputes or setting carbon-emission quotas. To counter US curbs on visit and immigration visas following 9/11, Yan demands that China embrace the opposite policy, although he does not necessarily explain how the PRC might deal with trans-national terrorism or, indeed, threats to the livelihood of its own menial laborers.

Strategic reliability will not extend to Japan, it seems. Unlike PLA persona like colonel Liu Mingfu, Yan's problem with Japan is, however, not primarily of a military bent. Rather, Japan is an agent of US soft power whose post-war democratization poses an ideological and cultural challenge; like Korea's or Taiwan's more recent democratization, this challenge is proving problematic for the CCP to acknowledge for obvious reasons (*Ancient Chinese Thought*, pp. 66–67, 245). That these East Asian democracies operate to different tunes is not much thought of in comparison with the CCP-favored Singaporean model. But the specter of Japanese history continues to haunt "China Model" intellectuals including Yan for yet another, much more pressing cause: they are concerned that without further economic reform and wiser foreign-policy, China would irreversibly slide into a Tokyoesque "Lost Decade" in the near future, whereby it might end up short of super-powerdom, and remain amenable to Washington.[28]

Yan knows that, unless China allows for more representative government, it will lose the fray domestically and internationally. Here, again, he enlists Xunzi: the latter was of course a great believer in rites and norms as validators of political power. Characteristically, Yan suggests that since democratization (broadly defined) has become an international norm, China will not be able to buck the trend if it were to effectively pursue global leadership.

One could only wish for future studies of this kind to elaborate from a more rigorous historic perspective on the hallmarks of what Axl Rose might flippantly dub "Chinese Democracy". On closer look, and contrary to conventional wisdom, it would appear that the term might potentially convey a broader meaning than CCP agit-prop or Heavy Metal allows for. My point here is that there were a few elements to China's past that

[28]Liu Mingfu (*Zhongguo meng*, trans. "The China Dream", published by Zhonghua shuju, 2010) rejects the notion that China can become a different kind of non-interventionist superpower, and calls for more resources to be poured into military build-up.

arguably made the imperial polity more egalitarian and socially mobile than pre-modern Europe. This is precisely where more collaboration between historians and political scientists is necessary in order to deepen our understanding of China's particularities.

One of the most compelling exemplars of the potentialities of "Chinese Democracy" is encapsulated perhaps in the Chinese idiom that is remarkably still in wide use even today: *fu bu guo sandai* ("wealth cannot last for more than three generations").

As explained by prominent Chinese sociologist and "China Model" thinker Pan Wei of Peking University, the historic sediments underlying the continued use of this expression speak to the relevance of China's past to China's future, as well as to the recognition that some universal values can assume different manifestations.[29] And yet, this aspect of Chinese imagery is rarely acknowledged in Western scholarship on contemporary China. To the contrary, the grip of corrupt Party princelings on China's economy is usually seized upon, whilst evidence for upward mobility across the CCP's different echelons is often dismissed off-hand. Yet, it would be difficult to understand the implications of humanity's timeless yearning for a "fair go" whilst neglecting its distinct Chinese expression.

Be that as it may, Yan then goes on to toe the official CCP line (pp. 219–221):

> Although China supports the one-party leadership of the Communist Party, it still retains the consultative system of having eight democratic parties, so the Chinese government proclaims that China is a multiparty state . . . China must make the moral principle of democracy one of those it promotes.

Yan's insipid depiction of democracy in this passage does a disservice to his otherwise profound and innovative thought on the historic "China Model". In some ways, it is a mirror image of US neo-conservatives who once simplistically thought, for example, that enforcing "democracy" in places like the Middle East would stabilize *Pax Americana* by definition. But the jury is still out on whether democracy in the developing world has

[29]On the resonance of *fu bu guo sandai* in contemporary PRC society, see e.g., "Reflections on the 'Consultative Rule of Law Regime': A Response to My Critics" by prominent political scientist and public intellectual Pan Wei. In S. Zhao (ed.), *Debating Political Reform in China: Rule of Law vs. Democratization* (M.E. Sharpe, 2006), pp. 247–254.

such healing qualities. In US academe, there were in turn many prominent professors who had prophesied the demise of the Chinese miracle time and again, whilst talking up democratic India's achievements. Harvard's Tarun Khanna who, for example, had lambasted the Chinese state owned sector earlier in his career has since changed his outlook; Khanna is now wondering in public how come the Chinese can build cities overnight with such poor corporate governance and lack of administrative transparency, whilst Indians keep voting into office politicians with criminal records in the face of media scrutiny (Khanna, 2007).[30]

One might further argue that whole construct of US engagement with China since 1971 had been informed by the catechism that free markets would inevitably lead to a more pro-Western outlook. And it was only late last year that Australia's Foreign Minister, Bob Carr, mustered the courage for the first time to state the obvious in Western ears: a more democratic China might actually turn out a more nationalistic China, at least in the short run, because the CCP keeps matters in check (*Australian Financial Review*, 2012).

Democracy aside, Yan's view that China's rise was perfectly predictable in view of the country's stature in pre-modern times (Chapter 4) might come across as somewhat facile. He thereby belittles at once the enormity of the challenges which China faced in 1978 *and* the catastrophes which the CCP was partly to blame for before 1978. On the one hand, Yan repeatedly levels criticism at George W. Bush's right-wing unilateralism. But, on the other hand, Yan's determinism is almost a precise mirror image of right-wing US views like, for example, that of Rudi Giuliani, who glorifies American global leadership as eternal in essence.[31]

Historians, on their part, know that every empire tends to think of itself as novel and as more benign toward its subjects than the one it had just brought down. US global leadership was no exception: it made a point of announcing itself at the turn of the 20th century as non-imperialistic,

[30]T. Khanna, *Billions of Entrepreneurs: How China and India Are Reshaping Their Futures-And Yours and Yours* (Harvard Business Press, 2007).

[31]For more detailed critique of Yan's determinism, see W. A. Callahan (2012). "Sino-speak: Chinese Exceptionalism and the Politics of History", *Journal of Asian Studies*, 71.1(2012): 33–55.

hence better and different than the "old" European powers (Bowden, 2009, pp. 189–214).[32] In other words, the US has messianically cast itself as a promoter of democracy, small government, and free markets worldwide — it is neither interested in colonies, nor satrapies. Yet, US intentions mean different things to different people even within the US itself, and the language of goodwill does not always carry. It sometimes takes a first-rate iconoclast like Iggy Pop to observe unapologetically: "America is Rome" (Pop, 1995).[33] When articulating their vision of a *new* kind of superpower — a non-interventionist one — it may be the case the thinkers like Yan might want to reflect on Pop's conclusion by substituting America for China.

Despite occasional inconsistency, whether readers ultimately find Yan a CCP conformist or daring intellectual innovator might depend on the degree they are willing to grant Chinese intellectual discourse the benefit of the doubt, and perhaps on their own pre-conceived ideas about China. Considering the tenor of public debate in the PRC, where one reader might trace inconsistency, another might find subtlety and daring. At times, inconsistency feeds onto originality to form a fascinating tapestry where timeless ideals as expressed in the classics and latter-day canon are interlaced with hard-nosed hyper-modern realism. Thus, in one of the rare passages where Mao's legacy is addressed, Yan can assert that (p. 62) the "... theory of perpetual revolution is a theory of the weak overcoming the strong, which has very strong universal potential and may be used for military conflict by many weak groups resisting powerful ones". Yet, several chapters later, Yan can scathingly damn Mao's Cultural revolution as having (pp. 250–251):

> ... gravely damaged China's traditional culture. I think that the greatest social danger in China today is hypocrisy. The Cultural Revolution destroyed the millennial ethical tradition of China: its sincerity ... If China wants to resolve the problem of counterfeiting, it must start by opposing the telling of lies.

In conclusion, it may be fair to say that most historians should find Yan's ideas stimulating if at times somewhat contradictory. Whether Zhanguo

[32] B. Bowden, *The Empire of Civilization: The Evolution of an Imperial Idea* (University of Chicago Press, 2009), pp. 189–214.

[33] I. Pop, "Caesar Lives", *Classic Ireland*, vol. 2 [online edition]. Available at: http://www.ucd.ie/cai/classics-ireland/1995/Pop95.html.

experts find the book true to their understanding of that era is for them to say. Either way, Yan is no doubt a great visionary whose work in Chinese and English has, at the very least, rendered that era much more significant to today's world than one might otherwise assume; *Ancient Chinese Thought, Modern Chinese Power* might prove the subject matter of future generations of scholars. Perhaps not the typical fare for economists, this book nonetheless adds a good deal more to the quality of the "China Model" discourse both among policy wonks and among social scientists.

Chapter 5

"Seoul Searching": The History, Politics, and Prejudice behind the Re-naming of the Korea's Capital in Chinese

Introduction

On January 19, 2005, Seoul Mayor at the time and later South Korea's president, Lee Myung Bak, held a press conference to announce his desire to see the Chinese name for Seoul changed from the traditional rendition of Hancheng (漢城) to Shouer (首爾). By explaining that the change was a matter of phonetic convenience — "Shouer" phonetically approximates the Korean sound of "Seoul", as opposed to "Hancheng" which bears no phonetic similarity whatsoever — Mayor Lee made clear that he was motivated by a simple desire to remove a potential cause for Sino-Korean "confusion". Lee further suggested that the principal beneficiary of the name-change would be those Chinese in some way connected to Seoul, and proclaimed that all signage carrying the Chinese characters for Hancheng would be changed accordingly, and that the traditional Chinese name would be promptly discontinued in South Korea.[1]

[1]Reported in the newspaper *Chosunilbo*, the most widely read newspaper in South Korea. Available at: http://news.chosun.com/svc/content_view/content_view.html?contid=2005011970127. This received attention from the major Japanese daily newspapers, including the *Asahi Shimbun* (February 9, 2005) and the *Nihon Keizai Shimbun* (February 10, 2005). This was also reported in *Xinhua*, the PRC official news agency. See http://news.xinhuanet.com/world/2005-01/19/content_2482227.htm; see also fairly laconic report in the traditional-character online edition http://www.people.com.cn/BIG5/guoji/14549/2530048.html.

If Mayor Lee had hoped for an uncontroversial re-naming, he was proven right for the most part. Not only did the Chinese government grant Mayor Lee's wish quickly and quietly, but regional media outlets also remained notably low-key on the naming issue. Lengthy editorial commentary on the matter on the front pages of either South Korean or Chinese (People's Republic of China (PRC)) newspapers does not exist; similarly, Japanese newspapers offered little more than the simple observation that Seoul's Chinese name had changed. As we will demonstrate below, there is nonetheless good reason to believe that Lee's move was driven by overarching concerns about China's growing regional clout, and that in this context, the character Han 漢 composing "Hancheng" could be potentially misrepresented as suggestive of ethnic-Han ownership of Seoul.

We believe, in addition, that the significance of Seoul's name-change in Chinese extends well beyond semantics, and can in a sense be seen as a test-case for the PRC's ability to leverage soft power in the region, and allay the concerns of its neighbors about the implications of its geo-strategic rise. The PRC has recently begun to semi-officially endorse the idea of re-establishing a Confucian "harmonious" cultural sphere in East Asia. Against this backdrop, we argue that China's willingness to accede to Seoul's name-change may be part of a new strategic thinking in Beijing, which posits "humane authority" (*wangdao* 王道) — namely establishing international authority by way of concessions and moral suasion — as key to pulling neighboring countries away from their reliance on the US military umbrella.[2] While the academic literature on Chinese soft power is extensive, this chapter is to our knowledge the first one in the English language to thoroughly address the issue through the prism of Seoul's name-change in Chinese.[3]

Though it is perfectly sound to question on what grounds Beijing would want to refuse Seoul's request at a time when China's so-called "charm offensive" was in full swing, we show in this chapter that it is wrong to deem the re-naming of Seoul a "no-cost" or merely perfunctory PRC gesture, considering the prominence of pre-modern semantics in ongoing territorial disputes across the region, and in view of the popular backlash such a

[2] See e.g., X. Yan, *Ancient Chinese Thought, Modern Chinese Power* (Princeton, 2011).
[3] See e.g., J. Kurlantzik, *Charm Offensive* (New Haven, 2007).

gesture could potentially arouse. After all, it is precisely historiography and semantics that foreground what many Chinese see as South Korean ambition to take over the North on the back of American military support and, once there, to let US soldiers man the border with China, and later carve up parts of Jilin Province where many ethnic Koreans reside. Conversely, South Koreans are often rattled precisely by what appears to them like a contrived PRC historic discourse that is designed to legitimize territorial claims on parts of what is today North Korea.[4]

To be sure, Chinese blogosphere is usually more nationalistic than Chinese government positions, and this case is no exception. By the same token, the Chinese government frequently overlooks grassroots xenophobia in framing polices toward Japan and the US, and thus a more moderate *official* language toward South Korea (ROK) can certainly be expected on a day-to-day basis. However, PRC pragmatism vis-à-vis the US or Japan rarely assume the same long-term historic-narrative implications that are manifest in Seoul's name-change, whilst defusing media attention elsewhere. Thus, for example, the 1979 neologism "Chinese Taipei" for Kuomintang-controlled Taiwan was a gesture the US helped coin so as to appease the PRC, not the other way around; and one that was not devoid of media coverage.[5]

Neither do we wish to overlook the major deterioration that occurred in Sino-ROK relations in 2010. Beijing's solitary refusal to condemn the North Korean sinking of the corvette Cheonan and Pyongyang's subsequent attack on the island of Yeonpyeong — the first military attack on South Korean territory since 1953 — triggered off anger across the ROK toward Beijing. China's continued refusal to exert serious pressure on North Korea to scale down its destabilizing military aggression has damaged China's standing in the ROK.

Yet, in construing overall PRC policy formulation vis-à-vis Lee's administration, one might well speculate that disappointment over the

---

[4] Z. Chen (2012). "Embracing the Complexities in China–ROK Relations: A View from China", *Asian Perspective*, April–June, 36(2), 195–218.

[5] C. K. Lin, "How 'Chinese Taipei' Came About", *Taipei Times*, published online on August 5, 2008. Available at: http://www.taipeitimes.com/News/editorials/archives/2008/08/05/2003419446.

latter's cool response to the gesture of re-naming Seoul in Chinese when still mayor; his subsequent abandonment of previous administrations' attempt at appeasing North Korea, as well his bold embrace of the US once entering the Blue House, have all converged to tilt Beijing closer toward Lee's center-left rivals at home.[6]

Inevitably, once the PRC refused to place the blame for sinking the Cheonan squarely on North Korea's shoulder, Lee sought to forge much greater strategic collaboration with the US to the extent that bilateral ties with China saw a further setback. But, if anything, the fact that Seoul's re-naming is virtually unmentioned even in lengthiest and most detailed scholarly treatments of the evolution of Sino-Korean ties should draw some attention to the subject rather than serve as a proof of its triviality. Indeed, the gravity of the issue at hand would seem compelling when hypothetically placed within other regional dynamics: consider, for example, how incendiary an Israeli government request from Ankara to change the former's capital appellation in Turkish from "Kudüs" to "Yerushalaim" might potentially be; or an Irish demand that the UK forbid its domestic media from using the term "Ulster"; or for that matter a UK demand that the French cease calling London "Londres".

Seoul in Korean History

During its long history, the city of Seoul has changed name some half-a-dozen times. It began as the capital city of one of the Korean peninsula's three historical kingdoms, known as Baekje (18 BC–660 AD). Situated north of the Han River (漢川), the city was called Wiryseong (위례성; 慰禮城). It soon moved, however, south of the Han River and was renamed Hanseong (한성; 漢城) according to the Korean sounds of the Chinese characters extensively used by Korean literati at the time, or Hancheng in the Chinese rendition of the same characters.[7] The city's name changed to Namgyeong (남경;

[6]G. Rozman (2012). "History as an Arena of Sino-Korean Conflict and the Role of the United States", *Asian Perspective*, April–June, 36(2): 278; S. W. Harold, "Beijing Unflustered by Cool Ties with Seoul", *YaleGlobal*, published online August 14, 2012. Available at: http://yaleglobal.yale.edu/content/beijing-unflustered-cool-ties-seoul.

[7]For the history of the early Baekje kingdom when it was based in the Seoul region, see G. R. Lee (ed.), *Wonbon Samguksagi* (The Original Version of the Samguk-sagi) (Seoul: Hangilsa, 1998), pp. 227–248.

南京) during the Goryeo dynasty (918–1392); it reverted back to Hanseong (or Hanyang) (한성; 漢城/한양; 漢陽) during the Joseon dynasty (1392–1910). Its name changed yet again to Gyeongseong (pronounced Keijō in Japanese; 경성; 京城) during the period of Japanese colonial rule (1910–1945), before changing to Seoul soon after World War II ended in 1945.

The Japanese in the early postwar period followed the dictates of their American occupiers and quickly adopted the new Korean name, Seoul (ソウル) which is based on the indigenous Korean term for capital city, and for which there have been no equivalent Chinese characters until recently. The Chinese, however, continued until 2005 to use the traditional name Hancheng (漢城). As a result, the Chinese name did not in any way approximate the Korean pronunciation of Seoul. The need to address this discrepancy provided the fulcrum across which South Korea's mainstream media reported on the name-change. Indeed, implicit in most accounts was a perceived prosaic need to prevent any possible confusion among Chinese about the Korean-ness of Seoul. In short, the South Korean media presented Seoul's name-change as being mainly of benefit to the Chinese.[8]

On balance, this was a show of real restraint on the part of the South Korean media. After all, as already mentioned, the name-change could have potentially been projected as a nationalist act of protection. It should also be noted that, only 12 months before the Chinese accepted Seoul's name-change, the South Korean media alluded to such nationalist sentiments. To provide but one example: the *Chosunilbo*, in August 2004 alleged that the Chinese were "unhappy" with efforts at a name-change because those efforts revealed a South Korean "independent streak". In this way, South Korea's most widely read daily newspaper linked the name-change with a separation from Chinese influence.[9]

Efforts at distinguishing clearly between Koreans and Chinese stretch far beyond the naming of Seoul into Korean medieval and early-modern history; ironically, such efforts were often instigated not by resentment of China but by underlying affinity. Indeed, as an integral part of what some have called the "Chinese interaction sphere",[10] Korea was — for very many

---

[8]http://news.chosun.com/svc/content_view/content_view.html?contid=2005011970127.

[9]http://news.chosun.com/svc/content_view/content_view.html?contid=2004081070258.

[10]K. C. Chang, "China on the Eve of the Historical Period", in M. Loewe and E. L. Shaughnessy (eds.), *The Cambridge History of Ancient China* (Cambridge: Cambridge University Press, 1999), pp. 37–73, in particular p. 59.

centuries — unashamedly Sinocentric. When Koreans spoke of *sadaejui* (or serving the great), they spoke of serving China. Indeed, Koreans went so far as to label their own society "little China", and after the fall of China's "legitimate" Ming dynasty and its takeover by the "barbarian" Manchus in the 17th century, the Yangban elite of the Joseon dynasty considered Korea to be the sole bastion of Chinese civilization (or rather, neo-Confucian civilization).[11] It was within this Sinocentric setting that the capital city of Hanseong/Hancheng emerged and thrived; there is every reason to believe that the Koreans themselves readily adopted a name connoting "Chinese city" (or Hancheng/Hanseong) for their own capital city in order to infuse it with an air of high civilization.[12]

This remarkable love for everything Chinese (which is somewhat mirrored in contemporary Korea by the love of all things Western) came to an abrupt halt in the late 19th and early 20th centuries, with the intrusions of the colonial powers and Imperial Japan. Indeed, by the 1950s, South Koreans no longer regarded China as the fountainhead of all civilization, but instead as poor, backward, communist country where supposedly uncouth "barbarians" (중국오랑캐) dwell. This rejection of most aspects of Chinese influence coincided with a distinct rise in Korean nationalism; that streak of nationalism was itself arguably tinged with racialism that attributed a pure genetic origin to all Koreans. It led among other things to an instinctive repugnance among South Koreans of being mistaken for Chinese by outsiders, or by the Chinese themselves.[13]

---

[11] J. H. Kim Haboush, *The Confucian Kingship in Korea: Yongjo and the Politics of Sagacity* (New York: Columbia University Press, 1988), pp. 21–28.

[12] For a very balanced analysis of the Joseon–China tributary relations and *Sadae* before the 19th century, see K. W. Larsen, *Tradition, Treaties and Trade: Qing Imperialism and Choson Korea, 1850–1910* (Cambridge MA: Harvard University Press, 2008), pp. 29–35.

[13] In this context, one has to consider, for example, the removal of references to Gija, the mythical Chinese "founder" of the nation, in history books in South Korea. D. Chen (2012). "Domestic Politics, National Identity, and International Conflict: The case of the Koguryo Controversy", *Journal of Contemporary China*, 21.74(March): 233. For a critique of this racialism in Korean historical scholarship, see H. I. Pai, *Constructing "Korean" Origins: A Critical Review of Archaeology, Historiography, and Racial Myth in Korean State-Formation Theories* (Cambridge MA and London: Harvard University Press, 2000). See also G. W. Shin, *Ethnic Nationalism in Korea: Genealogy, Politics, and Legacy* (Stanford CA: Stanford University Press, 2006).

China's rise over the last few decades has not necessarily dispelled all of these negative perceptions. Rather, it has elicited a Chinese politico-historic assertiveness, which has in turn escalated numerous Sino-Korean territorially-framed disputes. For example, recent Chinese claims to historic affinity with Koguryo 高句麗 and Balhae 渤海國 have run headlong into South Korea's own national discourse, which has long since held those two kingdoms to be incontrovertibly Korean.[14] South Koreans also feel non-plussed by the notion of historically Chinese "provincial" regimes, and Korea's inclusion therein. Semi-officially endorsed by the Chinese government — and actively supported by many Chinese academics — this notion applies (1) to those states or peoples historically under Chinese cultural influence, and (2) to those whose territory is contiguous with modern-day China. Perhaps unsurprisingly, such ideas have served to convince many South Koreans that China is chauvinistic, imperialistic, paternalistic, and possibly even aggressive in its outlook.[15]

---

[14]For detailed analyses of this dispute over Koguryo and its significance, see P. Hays Gries (2005). "The Koguryo Controversy, National Identity, and Sino-Korean Relations today", *East Asia*, 22.4(Winter 2005): 3–17, and D. Chen, "Domestic Politics, National Identity, and International Conflict": 227–241. See also http://www.japanfocus.org/-Andrei-Lankov/2233 and http://www.japanfocus.org/-Yonson-Ahn/2631. For excellent analyses of the dispute over ancient history between China and South Korea and the negative effects of nationalist indoctrination in both countries, see G. H. Song, *East Asia's History Conflict* (Seoul: Sol Press, 2007), pp. 13–44; S. S. Lee, *Mandeul eo jin godeh: geun-deh gukmingukga ui Dongasia iyagi* (*Created Antiquity: The Early Modern Nation-State's Story of East Asia*) (Seoul: Samin, 2001), pp. 19–34, 186–188; J. O. Lee, *Goguryeo ui Yoksa* (*The History of Goguryeo*) (Seoul: Gimyoungsa, 2005), pp. 12–23. This highly publicized and acrimonious dispute between China and Korea over ancient history is also mirrored by an equally acrimonious disagreement over more recent history between Korea and Japan which receives treatment in K. Kazuhiko, "The Continuing Legacy of Japanese Colonialism: The Japan–South Korea Joint Study Group on History Textbooks", in L. Hein and M. Selden (eds.), *Censoring History: Citizenship and Memory in Japan, Germany, and the United States* (Armonk, NY: M.E. Sharpe, 2000), pp. 203–225.

[15]For a sound critique of this pseudo-historical approach, see Q. E. Wang, *Inventing China through History: The May Fourth Approach to Historiography* (Albany, NY: State University of New York Press, 2001), p. 121. See also K. C. Chang (2001). "Reflections on Chinese Archaeology in the Second Half of the Twentieth Century", *Journal of East Asian Archaeology*, 3.1–3.12(2001): 5–13.

In view of such perceptions, it is little wonder that *contemporary* South Koreans continue in their efforts to clearly distinguish "Korean" from "Chinese". The re-naming of "Seoul" perhaps ought to be seen against this backdrop. If so, it would not be at all unreasonable to expect the renaming issue to have inflamed nationalist passions in South Korea despite the low-key nature of the mainstream media coverage. Yet, not only did the renaming issue escape significant comment in South Korea's mainstream media, it also did relatively little to fire the imaginations of South Korea's netizens. Indeed, South Korean bloggers maintained almost complete silence on the issue. This stands in stark contrast to the vocal debate which the renaming issue sparked among Chinese and even Japanese netizens, as discussed further below; it is, therefore, entirely appropriate to question the reasons for South Koreans' silence.

We would suggest three factors at play. First, the demise of Classical Chinese as a written medium in contemporary Korea has minimized the exposure of the Korean public to this name-change in Chinese. In other words, it seems entirely possible that many Koreans have come to regard this as a "foreign" issue, or that the issue was locally and somewhat ironically de-sensitized because Chinese characters are much less understood nowadays.

Second, South Korea's reluctance to associate nationalism with this issue, which contrasts strikingly with the rather demeaning condescension that characterized Korean attitudes toward the Chinese in the recent past, surely has something to do with the rise of China over the past two decades.[16] China is now no longer the "backwards, poor" country that it used to be and this new found wealth and power of the Chinese has arguably contributed to the mellowing of Korean attitudes toward the Chinese. Money and power bring respect as always!

The third reason is closely tied up with the second. The rise of China has to some degree boosted left-wing alignments in Korea that tone down

[16]For a good analysis of this rise and what it implies, see C. Horner, *Rising China and its Postmodern Fate: Memories of Empire in a New Global Context* (Athens, Georgia: The University of Georgia Press, 2009), pp. 1–21, 145–156, 183–191. For the history of the evolution of South Korea–China diplomatic and economic relations, see J. H. Chung, *Between Ally and Partner: Korea–China Relations and the United States* (New York: Columbia University Press, 2007).

identity politics insofar as China can be portrayed as the antidote.[17] The established Korean left, which had historically favored communist North Korea and communist China and displayed a persistent anti-American and anti-Japanese approach, also has influential allies in the Korean media, who usually tone down the rhetoric or are silent when affairs that would present China negatively to the Korean public appear.[18] This pro-Chinese stance among the influential left-wing South Koreans and also the fear of the Korean business elite that any antagonism caused by excessive nationalistic outbursts may harm their interests in the PRC, have all contributed to the softening of the nationalist voice in the mass media.

[17]The intense polarization of Korean politics has forced us to use the rather outdated terms left and right instead of the more neutral terminology favored by the current Korean political establishment: Progressive and Conservative. See G. Rozman, "South Korea's National Identity Sensitivity", pp. 2–6, for discussion on the "Progressive" vs. "Conservative" conflict in Korean politics. The new terms are obviously borrowed from American politics. However, the weakness or virtual non-existence of any centrist parties in Korea is one of the peculiarities of Korean politics and quite obviously the residue of the cold war polarization that still divides the Korean peninsula. The two main parties Senuri (right-wing or conservative), Tonghap Minju (left-wing or progressive), are by no means the traditional center right or center left parties that we are familiar with in Western democracies. The outdated ideological conflicts that still govern the thinking of both parties warrant the use of the terms left and right when referring to them. Other political parties both on the left and right are even more radical than the two major parties mentioned above, which somewhat explains the extreme verbal and physical abuse that often blight the Korean parliament. For the recent "tear gas incident" in the Korean parliament where a far left MP threw tear gas at his rivals, a world first in parliamentary politics (!), see http://news.chosun.com/site/data/html_dir/2011/11/24/2011112400200.html and http://www.hani.co.kr/arti/politics/politics_general/510352.html. Tonghap Minju party has recently changed its name yet again to 새정치민주연합 (The New Politics Alliance for Democracy Party).

[18]*Gyeonghyang Sinmun* (경향신문), *Ohmy News* (오마이뉴스), *Hangyeoreh Sinmun* (한겨레신문), *MBC News network*, *Pressian* (프레시안), *Media Today* (미디어오늘), etc., all favor the left of the political spectrum and have shown a marked reluctance to criticize either the North Koreans or their Chinese patrons in Beijing. In contrast, their criticisms of the US and Japan have been extremely vigorous. Most of the news agencies cited above for instance denied the North Korean involvement in the recent Chonanham tragedy and rapidly adopted the Chinese official position toward the incident while rejecting the position espoused by the South Korean government and most of the international community. Their influence among the younger generation of Koreans is also very strong and will in all likelihood contribute to the growing support for Chinese interests among younger Koreans in the future. MBC News Network was predominantly left-wing until recently, but has now become more neutral.

Last but not least amongst the factors that could arguably account for Korea's low-key approach to name-change — or for the silence in the Korean blogosphere — is the fact the Chinese government fairly swiftly acceded to Mayor Lee's request. We would argue that the Chinese official reaction to Lee's request was astute because it helped stem the escalation of mutual suspicion carrying over from the historic disputes over "ownership" of the Koguryo and Balhae kingdoms.

The Chinese Reaction

Official PRC coverage of Seoul's name-change remained consistently low-key, as was the case with South Korea's mainstream media. Probably because the Chinese Communist Party (CCP) had decided in principle to accede to Lee Myung Bak's request, and in view of the nationalist backlash it might have unleashed, there seems to be intentionally little content in its leading mouthpieces that might elicit reactions in Zhongnanhai, or excite public attention. In what follows, we will therefore focus on unofficial sources in a bid to gage what might have gone through the minds of China's leaders as they weighed up Lee's request.

Such rationale for the name-change as Lee's might have conceivably raised in Chinese eyes the specter of demands for name changes of other historic cities across East Asia whose pronunciation in Mandarin is far-removed from the phonetics by which they are known elsewhere, e.g., Dongjing for Tokyo. However, as indicated above, the PRC official media did not openly question Lee's rationale. Furthermore, by the end of 2005, most media outlets in Taiwan, Hong Kong, Singapore, and other parts of the Sinophone world had chosen to follow Beijing's lead and reverted to "Shouer" *in lieu* of "Hancheng".

Notably, however, the traditional-character online edition of *Xinhua*, which is aimed at Taiwan readers in the main, did carry an op-ed piece by Mainland-born commentator Wong Ping Fah 黃彬華 published that day in Singapore's *Lianhe Zaobao* 聯合早報, and titled "Why Is Seoul's Name Change So Perplexing?".[19] Wong caustically remarked that Mayor Lee's move was one-sided, namely, directed *not* at Koreans, but in effect dictating

[19]http://big5.xinhuanet.com/gate/big5/news.xinhuanet.com/overseas/2005-02/04/content_2547303.htm.

to the Sinophone world that it drop a place name that had been in use for 600 years. Wong also alluded to the fact that Korea had for some time actually considered moving its capital to a new location in the middle of the country to be named Sejong in honor of the 15th-century king who created Hangul, the indigenous Korean alphabet. The relocation plan had been partly motivated by a desire to place government beyond the range of North Korean missiles, but it did not materialize.[20]

And yet — Wong noted — even though the capital relocation did not eventuate, a name-change of some sort was still required to allay Korean suspicions. While acknowledging foreigners had no right to "stick their beak" (*zhihui* 置喙) into how Koreans want to call their own capital city, Wong nonetheless wondered if Lee had the right to make such a diplomatically-sensitive request on behalf of the Korean central government, given that he was merely elected as mayor. Wong also questioned Lee's rationale on the grounds that many prominent foreign place name in modern Chinese are figurative rather than phonetically-constructed, e.g., San Francisco (*Jiujinshan* 舊金山, "Old Gold Mountain"), Honolulu (*Tanxiangshan* 檀香山, "Fragrant Sandalwood Mountain"), Cambridge (*Jianqiao* 劍橋, "Sword Bridge"), and Oxford (*Niujin* 牛津, "Ox Stream"), etc. After all, Wong concluded, it was the Korean Yi dynasty that enshrined in 1394 the specific characters for Hancheng, not a Chinese invasion of the country.

Quite predictably, Taiwan's pan-green (i.e., pro-independence) press depicted Lee's move more favorably. The *Liberty Times* 自由時報, for example, quoted Taiwanese Korea specialist Lin Chiu-shan 林秋山 who explained that the neologism Shouer would be in line with pronunciation in the rest of the world, reflecting the cosmopolitan nature of the city. But Lin added that Korea did have some unresolved psychological issues (*xinjie* 心結) concerning China, as borne out by the aforementioned historiographic disputes over how "Sinified" the medieval kingdoms of Koguryo and Balhae were. The same article also quoted the Korean Sinologist Ŏm Ik-sang (嚴翼相), who had been involved in the search committee for a new Chinese name for Seoul on behalf of the Mayor; Ŏm pleaded in the article that Lee's move was *not* political in nature. Rather, he infused the Mayor's request

[20]On the fate of capital relocation to Sejong see, e.g., D. Normile (2010). "New Korean Science City Caught in Political Crossfire", *Science*, February 5, 327(5966): 630.

with the aura of Confucian legitimacy that could potentially resonate with many Chinese when he described it as an attempt at "rectification of names" (*zhengming* 正名).[21]

Elsewhere in Greater China, Hong Kong's leading Chinese daily *Singtao* 星島 reported dryly on Lee's rationale of avoiding confusion among tourists. It also suggested that most Chinese residents of Seoul opposed the change despite official South Korean claims to the contrary.[22] The *Epoch Times* 大紀元, published by the nationalistic anti-Communist Buddhist sect known as Falungong, reported on February 27, 2005 that leading mainland newspapers like *Renmin ribao* (*People's Daily*) had already reverted to Shouer. However, the *Epoch Times* suggested that the Taiwanese press and government organs were somewhat less cooperative that their Mainland counterparts, even though Taipei was Seoul's sister city.[23] In fact, three days earlier, the *Epoch Times* had reported in a seemingly unrelated piece that semi-official Korean organizations expressed anger at the fact that an official Chinese government website used the term "Japan Sea" instead of "Eastern Sea" on its maps. The latter incident has indeed aroused rebuke in South Korea, which contrasts with the low-key approach to the name-change.[24] We would suggest that the use of the term "Japan Sea" by an official Chinese government website may not have been incidental, as claimed, but perhaps a trial retaliation to Lee's request by Beijing, which was ultimately abandoned thereby averting further escalation in bilateral relations.

Taiwanese blogosphere seemed by and large more restrained toward the name-change than PRC netizens. Many suggested Shouer sounded, indeed, more cosmopolitan. Lapsing into Hoklo slang perhaps intentionally, one pan-green blog even went as far as suggesting that Lee's move effectively countered PRC historiographic "bullying" (*lishishang de "yaba"* 歷史上的鴨霸), while conceding at the same time that on a personal level, the name-change was an inconvenience to speakers of Chinese.[25]

---

[21] http://www.libertytimes.com.tw/2005/new/jan/20/today-t1.htm.

[22] http://www.singtao.com/archive/fullstory.asp?andor=or&year1=2005&month1=1&day1=20&year2=2005&month2=1&day2=20&category=all&id=20050120b02&keyword1=&keyword2.

[23] http://www.epochtimes.com/b5/5/2/27/n829620.htm.

[24] http://www.epochtimes.com/b5/7/2/24/n1629155.htm.

[25] http://tw.myblog.yahoo.com/liaoran-lab/article?mid=3.

PRC bloggers conveniently overlooked, by and large, the fact that North Korea had actually discontinued the use of Chinese characters much earlier and more effectively than South Korea. Instead, many bloggers accused South Korea — under right-wing President Roh Tae-woo at the time — of intentionally expunging all trace of Chinese characters in the country ahead of the 1988 Seoul Olympics Games. Allegedly, when the left-wing President Kim Dae-jung tried in 1999 to lift some of the restriction on Chinese character use, Korean ultra-nationalists obstructed his move. The Shouer initiative was thus interpreted by many as simply the continuation of the sort of Korean jingoism that was unleashed in late 1980s.[26]

Arguably, one the most jingoistic entries in the PRC blogosphere suggested that Seoul's name-change was in fact part of a bigger South Korean plot, concocted in concert with the US, to make territorial claims on Northeast China (formerly Manchuria) on the grounds that it has been historically and ethnically Korean; Washington, it was alleged, aimed at destabilizing CCP rule, so that the two Koreas can then unify under American tutelage and expand east. Korea was depicted by this blog as possessing obsequious "vassal" (*weixingguo* 衛星國) mentality — first toward China; after 1910 toward Japan, and currently toward the US. But, the anonymous contributor warned, Korea was now acting blindly: client states cannot lean on one great power to provoke another great power for long, because they will crumble (*daomei* 倒霉) once the global balance of power shifts; truly crafty client states like Singapore or King Hussein's Jordan were successful and long-lasting, it was alleged, precisely because they were chary of provoking contending powers.[27]

Another anonymous PRC blogger suggested that the process of de-Sinification (*qu Zhongguo hua* 去中國化) in Korea had started — just like in Taiwan — as late as the 1980s, on the back of rapid economic

---

[26]http://www.city363.com/asia/seoul/531.htm. On the Roh era in Korean politics, see e.g., R. E. Bedeski and J. R. Brown, *The Transformation of South Korea: Reform and Reconstitution in the Sixth Republic under Roh Tae Woo, 1987–1992* (Routledge, 1994). On the history of written-language reform in East Asia more generally, see Wm. C. Hannas, *Asia's Orthographic Dilemma* (University of Hawai'i Press, 1997).

[27]http://bbs.tiexue.net/post_1462569_1.html.

modernization, and against the backdrop of relative poverty in China at the time. By contrast — the blogger alleged — Korea had been trying to look thoroughly Sinified for hundreds of years beforehand, in order to gain respect in the region. This particular blog aroused many talk-back responses, a few abusive in nature. One was eerily reminiscent of European post-war "Kraut-bashing":[28]

> Kimchi-land is talking tough again? As I said to my close friend, after you've eaten too much pickled cabbage you might become paranoid".
>
> 泡菜國又發威了?　我已經和很多身邊的朋友說過了泡菜吃多了,會發妄想症的。

From blogger abuse, we must now turn to equally germane yet more nuanced discussions in the PRC para-academic literature. Here, perhaps the most interesting commentary was by Liu Wansheng, a lecturer at the Foreign Languages Department of Nantong Vocational College. Published in a peripheral academic journal as late as 2008, Liu ambitiously deployed Foucault's power discourse theory in order to explain why South Korea might wish to change its capital's name in Chinese. He concluded that Korea scrambled to affirm the distinctiveness of its national culture by pitting it against what it saw as a hegemonic Sinitic culture. Echoing similar attitudes in blogosphere, Liu suggested that the Korean rush for national affirmation betrayed quite a reasonable urge to cash in on the country's relative economic advancement vis-à-vis neighboring China before it fades away. But Liu also asserted that Seoul's name-change was ultimately contrived (*qianqiang* 牵强), thereby divulging Korea's deep-seated cultural "cringe". At the same time, Liu contrasted that historically-grounded Korean "cringe" with the more recent wave of adulation for Korean (or Koreanized) pop-culture idols (*Hanliu* 韓流) among many PRC urban youths, particularly singers like Rain and Zhang Lala or actor Bae Yong Joon; Liu noted with bemusement the high ratings, which television dramas like Dae Jang Geum 大長今, set as they are in pre-modern Korea, can achieve in modern China. Finally, Liu speculated that China's last decade of breakneck economic progress might soon start to offset Chinese adulation for Korean

---

[28]http://www.tianya.cn/publicforum/content/worldlook/1/155653.shtml.

pop-culture, particularly as so many young Koreans study Mandarin in PRC universities.[29]

In a slightly revised version of the same article, published in 2009, Liu added that the strategists of China's rise should in fact learn from the Korean cultural experience and turn relative weakness to international strength. He described how three decades of economic reform and opening up to the West have turned English into the hegemonic language in the PRC, so much so that the rich sediments of Soviet cultural influence of the 1950s–1960s had been all but erased. Nonetheless, Liu thought that the hegemony of English can be effectively resisted by advancing Chinese culture onto the world stage. In practical terms, to learn from Seoul's name-change episode would require, according to Liu, that China insist other countries refer to Chinese national symbols by their Mandarin pronunciation, e.g., "Chinese Long" for "Chinese Dragon", "Kongzi" for Confucius, or "Jinngju" instead of Peking Opera. Liu stated that China needed to continue promoting Mandarin internationally through Confucius Institutes, and employ as many staff dedicated to the showcasing of Chinese culture as those dedicated to the instruction of English worldwide.[30]

Even if somewhat less inflammatory than blogosphere content, journals aimed at younger readership carried pieces much less appreciative of Korea's language policies. Under the pseudonym Chi Cheng 馳騁 ("galloping"), one author stood out as an exception to that pattern of moderation. In a 2005 piece, Chi Cheng fulminated that China was being "attacked" by Koreans on "every corner"; Korean culture was "taking over" the young through *Hanliu*, which despite some admittedly good-quality features was nonetheless infused with Korean supremacism; peddlers from North Korea were "everywhere" selling "South Korean"-labeled Kimchi with impunity, and Korean-made household appliances and automobiles proved all the rage. But this adulation for Korean culture only bred — according to

[29]W. Liu 劉万生 (2008). "Cong 'Hancheng' dao 'Shouer': wenhua qianshi diwei de kewang", *Anhui zhiye jishu xueyuan xuebao*, (3). On the impact of *HanLiu* and Korean pop music across East Asian, see also K. Lee, "Mapping Out the Cultural Politics of the 'Korean Wave' in Contemporary South Korea", in B. H. Chua and K. Iwabuchi (eds.), *East Asian Pop Culture* (Hong Kong University Press, 2008), pp. 157–172.

[30]W. Liu 劉万生 (2009). "Cong 'Hancheng' dao 'Shouer': jingji fazhan gaibian huayuquan", *Yibin xueyuan xuebao*, (3).

Chi Cheng — contempt for China among most Koreans, as shown by the ditching of "Hancheng", even when it was the ancestors of Koreans themselves who had embraced these two characters to denote Seoul. Chi Cheng then satirically suggested that all Koreans ought to change the sounds of their surnames if they were serious about rinsing themselves of Chinese culture, as these surnames were invariably derived from Chinese characters. He concluded in a retaliatory manner by asserting that Korea's was in fact an indistinct (*sibuxiang* 四不像) culture that borrowed all too heavily from China over the centuries, as compared with Japan's more genuinely syncretic nature.[31]

By contrast, in a 2005 piece, Zhou Yongsheng coolly suggested that Korea had every right to change place-name signage domestically. But, Zhou immediately added, it was up to the Sinophone world to decide whether it wished to accept the name-change outside Korea.[32] Mao Haiyan, a Chinese academic based in Korea, was even more accommodating. In a piece published in 2005, she suggested that the Koreans had a right to change the name of their capital in Chinese irrespective of the rationale of such a change. Seemingly dismissive of the uproar elsewhere, Mao concluded that the induction of Shouer *in lieu* of Hancheng was not much different to the PRC's insistence that Westerners re-spell Peking as Beijing earlier on.[33] Quan Yinchu similarly countenanced the name-change in broad terms even while acknowledging it would put the Sinophone world to great trouble (*mafan* 麻煩). For Quan, the ultimate vindication for the name-change was the fact that Japan, too, had resorted to Katakana phonetics in order to denote Seoul rather than clinging to the traditional Chinese characters.[34]

Pieces like Mao's and Quan's were filliped by interviews with Korean scholars published in other Chinese journals. In one such interview, South Korean sinologist Meng Joo-Oeck (孟柱亿), for example, re-iterated at length that the name-change was in the main phonetic in nature — it

---

[31] Chi Cheng 驰骋 (2005). "Bu guan 'Hancheng' jiao 'Shouer'", *Shaonian rensheng* (Youth Life), (21).

[32] Y. Zhou 周永生 (2005). "Hancheng gaiming 'Shouer' wei naban", *Tangzheng luntan*, (4).

[33] H. Mao 毛海燕 (2005). " 'Hancheng' gaiwei 'Shouer' zhihou", *Dangdai Hanguo*, (4).

[34] Y. Quan 全寅初 (2005). "Hanguo shoudu Hanzi biaoji you 'Hancheng' gaiwei 'Shouer' ", *Dangdai Hanguo*, (1).

was concerned with bringing Seoul's pronunciation in Mandarin closer to the Korean original, and with avoiding confusion. Much like the aforementioned Ŏm Ik-sang, Meng tried to play down historiographic disputes between the two countries by invoking the Confucian term *zhengming* as precondition for good governance. Meng then reminding his Chinese interlocutors that the PRC, too, had changed South Korea's name in Mandarin from Nan Chaoxian 南朝鲜 to the less confrontational Hanguo 韩国 after the establishment of diplomatic relations in 1992; it was now only natural, *pace* Meng, to further facilitate bilateral relations by prizing Shouer over Hancheng.[35]

The Japanese Reaction

The Japanese are no strangers to name-changes within their region. The Japanese Government from the mid-19th century took to referring to China in more minimalist terms as "Shinkoku" (清国) or "Qing-dynasty Country" instead of the more traditional "Middle Kingdom" (*Chūgoku* 中国); by the early 20th century, Japanese officials favored the somewhat pejorative term "Shina" (支那); and soon after World War II, the Japanese preference switched right back to Chūgoku (中国).[36]

As indicated above, throughout the period of Japanese colonial rule over the Korean peninsula, Seoul was known not by its traditional Sinitic name of Hancheng (漢城) but instead as Keijō/Gyeong Seong (京城). When US occupation authorities in Korea in the early aftermath of World War II declared that the capital's correct name was "Seoul", the Japanese (themselves under US occupation) simply abandoned the use of Chinese characters and reverted to the Katakana phonetic syllabary, so that the sounds of the South Korean capital became approximated as Souru (ソウル).

Yet, if the mainstream media remains an accurate barometer of public opinion, then it seems fair to assert that the issue was of little interest to most Japanese. Such major dailies as *Asahi Shimbun* and *Nihon Keizai*

---

[35]J. O. Meng 孟柱亿 (2005). "Cheng 'Hancheng' wei 'Shouer' bus hi gaiming, er shi zhengming", *Zhejiang wanli xueyuan xuebao*, (4).

[36]See especially J. A. Fogel, *The Cultural Dimension of Sino-Japanese Relations: Essays on the Nineteenth and Twentieth Centuries* (Armonk, NY: M.E. Sharpe, 1995), pp. 66–78.

Shimbun (or *Nikkei*, as it is popularly known) did, to be sure, carry stories explaining the name-change; these were nonetheless brief, matter-of-fact, and devoid of opinion or comment.[37] The principal cause of this Japanese lack of interest is readily discernible: this was a Sino-Korean issue, and Japan remained a bystander.

Of course, not all Japanese professed equanimity. The issue animated the blogosphere, even if only for a short time. Many Japanese netizens felt the name Hancheng (漢城) was indicative of a — real or imagined — Chinese mindset, which clings to the notion of itself being "suzerain" or "overlord" of the region.[38] Drawing such thinking to its logical conclusion, one blogger congratulated the Korean people soon after the Chinese consented to Seoul's name-change. In a rather obvious state of excitement, he wrote: "You can now say in triumph that Korea is not China's tributary state!"[39] As if to highlight the spectrum of ideas and opinions informing the Japanese, one right-wing blogger reached an altogether different conclusion, and saw reason not to congratulate but to belittle the South Koreans. "Maybe Koreans, who cannot read Chinese characters", he wrote, "do not know their own origins".[40]

Other bloggers related the issue directly back to Japan. One blogger saw China's perceived antagonism to the name-change as being analogous to the well-known Chinese practice of pronouncing Japanese names in accord *not* with their Japanese reading but with the Chinese reading (the cited instance being Prime Minister Tanaka Kakuei, who in the 1970s normalized Japan's relations with China, but who in China was known as "Tianzhong" rather than Tanaka).[41] Another blogger angrily questioned why the Chinese would accede to Korean requests regarding Seoul, but continue to refer to the Japanese Prefecture of Okinawa as "the *Liuqiu* 琉球 Islands".[42]

Tanaka Nobuhiko wrote what was perhaps one of the more thoughtful accounts to come out of the Japanese blogosphere. A lecturer in Asia

[37] *Asahi Shimbun*, February 9, 2005; *Nihon Keizai Shimbun*, February 10, 2005.
[38] http://blog.goo.ne.jp/noridar002/e/f88472796468682acc8a1af7f2912e22.
[39] http://blog.livedoor.jp/wildhorse38/archives/50155793.html.
[40] http://tosi.iza.ne.jp/blog/entry/796538/.
[41] http://blogs.dion.ne.jp/bunsuke/archives/529787.html.
[42] http://sh.explore.ne.jp/yorozu/45087_1.html.

University's Graduate School of Asian and International Business Strategy, Tanaka acknowledged that the literal meaning of Hancheng (漢城 "Chinese city") was probably distasteful for many Koreans. He added, however, that most Chinese had probably never considered the literal meaning of Hancheng. It only had meaning because, he averred, this was "how the Chinese have long since named Seoul". Tanaka came out explicitly in favor of the status quo, which of course meant he favored retention of the name "Hancheng".[43]

Tanaka then turned his attention to Sino-Japanese relations, and made an interesting comparison. Reminding his readers that the Chinese call Tokyo "Dongjing", he asked: "Do we tell China: 'Tokyo is not Dongjing. It is Tokyo.' If it comes to that, then the Japanese will have to stop saying 'Peking' and instead use 'Beijing'. . . It would, in fact, require the writing of Chinese place names not in Chinese characters but instead in Katakana (Japanese phonetic syllabary)". He concluded with the thought that, in his mind at least, the use of Chinese characters rather than Katakana had two great advantages. It was (1) "more beautiful", and (2) respectful of Sino-Japanese "shared culture".[44]

Conclusions

The analysis of the official and unofficial media and academic responses to the name-change in China, South Korea, and Japan yields numerous fascinating perspectives. One of the most noticeable trends in the Chinese discourse on the name-change is the desire among the wider Chinese public for the re-assertion of China's dominant political and cultural role in the East Asia region, and frustration at Lee Myung Bak's apparent disregard for the inconvenience of phasing out an age-old place name in Chinese. On the extreme, the name-change was viewed in some instances rather disturbingly as the "revolt" and "impertinent self-assertion" of a former "vassal" state. The venom with which some Chinese bloggers have reacted to the name-change is indicative of the newly assertive and at time jingoistic mood of certain segments of Chinese society. Quite obviously, the PRC government

---

[43] http://www.actiblog.com/tanaka/40102.
[44] *Ibid.*

had chosen on this occasion to avoid confrontation and wisely keep jingoism at bay by rapidly agreeing to the Korean requests for the name-change, and maintaining low-key coverage of the issue in the state-run media.

However, it is evident that there is a growing number of Chinese who are no longer in the mood for any perceived "concessions". This will likely mean increasing difficulties in the future for Chinese policy-makers who will struggle to cope with the rising nationalist sentiment of their people while striving to pursue a more pragmatic foreign policy toward the rest of East Asia.

Yet, the speedy, quiet, and effective resolution of the name-change issue is an indication that common sense has prevailed among China's diplomats and leaders over nationalist pressures. Moreover, it is an indication that historically-hued semantics, i.e., the politics of naming neighborly localities, can potentially be deployed to allay suspicion of China's intent just as it is an all-to-familiar channel for inflaming popular sentiments. Will such common sense among China's leaders sufficiently contain the popular fervor currently arising as a result of the escalating territorial dispute surrounding the Diaoyutai/Senkaku and Spratly Islands? That remains to be seen. What will be the impact of nationalist sentiments further afield, as China continues to global cachet?[45]

The foregoing analysis of popular reactions to the name-change in all three countries thus poses some serious questions about the retention of stability in East Asia. But, perhaps more importantly, the accession to Mayor Lee's request by the Chinese government speaks to the benign potential of newly-envisioned theoretical principles such as "humane authority" if and when they are applied to modern PRC foreign policy.

The picture that emerges from the observation of Korean reactions to the name-change is also highly complex. On the one hand, Lee Myung Bak's name-change initiative bespeaks widely-shared nationalist sentiments and deep-seated suspicion of Chinese intent. Yet, on the other hand, the political fault-lines that divide Korean society are still quite strong. The fear among Koreans, particularly those of right-wing leanings, of an increasingly powerful China is often implicit rather than explicitly stated. It may well be

[45]For a broader discussion of how public opinion impact on PRC policy, see e.g., J. Reilly, *Strong Society, Smart State* (Columbia University Press, 2012).

the case that the South Korean low-key approach to Seoul's name-change, as well as the subsequent accession by the Chinese government to name-change request, could signal a new *modus operandi* of resolving bilateral disputes and ultimately securing closer relations quite apart from which side of South Korean politics is in power.

Similarly, the virtual silence in the Korean media about the name-change might reveal the extent to which established and new left-wing alignments could mitigate popular perceptions of China or, indeed, the degree to which South Korea wishes to remain in the US fold and at loggerheads with North Korea. Yet, sooner or later, a more overtly pro-Chinese stance by Korean intellectual elites will be called into question again over issues of historiographic (read: symbolic) or substantive significance. How South Korea's right-wing politicians will reconcile the bipartisan imperative of keeping China — nowadays their country's largest trading partner — on side with the underlying popular suspicion of China in South Korea remains to be seen.

The analysis of the Japanese approach to the name-change has likewise revealed growing anxiety over China's rise, even if a few comments valorized the shared Sino-Japanese cultural baggage. The generally favorable response and even support for Korea's decision to assert its "independence" reflects the desire to maintain the current balance of power in East Asia, which would be perturbed if the Koreans were to shift their allegiance to China and sever ties with their American and Japanese allies. There remains, however, an underlying current of ambivalence toward Korea, as revealed by those netizens who took the occasion to belittle and deride Seoul's name-change.

At the heart of all this is lingering mistrust among East Asian nations toward each other areas — yet unresolved territorial disputes that continue to muddy popular and elite perceptions. To these factors, one should add the great uncertainty across the region about the viability of North Korea. The largely pro-Chinese sentiment of South Korean left-wing political parties and their supporters may not be enough to contain the nationalist uproar that may erupt if China chooses to intervene actively in North Korean affairs in order to prevent its disintegration or "fall" into American hands.

In that sense, it would appear that South Korea might have some soul-searching to do in terms of genuinely re-defining its national identity and determining where its strategic future lies, quite apart from searching for a new Chinese name for Seoul. Has the relatively quiet acceptance of "Shouer" paved the way to closer Sino-Korean relations? Or are we likely to see President Lee or even Prime Minister Noda demanding sometime in the near future that Renchuan 仁川 (Incheon) and Dongjing (Tokyo), too, be re-named in Chinese? As was argued throughout this chapter, such questions extend well beyond semantics even if they are not immediately provoked by the ethnocentric connotation of the character Han 漢. To a great extent, in fact, these seemingly semantic concerns encapsulate what the future may have in store for the region; it is a future where — we argue — pragmatic concerns might end up offsetting the ironically divisive potential of shared East Asian history, culture, and language. On balance, we would thus cautiously suggest that the top-down "Shouer" formula is one that could bode well for conflict resolution between the governments of the region in the face of lingering popular suspicion.

Chapter 6

Is My Rival's Rival a Friend? Popular Third-Party Perceptions of Territorial Disputes in East Asia

Introduction

China's resurgence on the world stage has clearly manifested itself over the past year in a much bolder stance toward Japan. Partly in response to the Japanese state purchase of the Senkaku/Diaoyutai Islands, a boycott of Japanese goods swept across China, seriously affecting bilateral economic relations. While much attention, for example in the media, throughout this ongoing territorial dispute has been devoted to official positions and interactions, this chapter instead focuses on the unmediated seam of *popular* animosity between the two countries as expressed online in blogs. Furthermore, the issue will *not* be conventionally explored through the prism of Sino-Japanese exchanges, which have already received much attention.[1]

Rather, we will seek in the main to examine how China's rise and increasing tensions with Japan are portrayed by South Korean bloggers. We do that as part of a broader research agenda which seeks to elucidate third-party popular perceptions of territorial disputes across East Asia. In other words, we are primarily interested to know how deterioration in relations between China and Japan might project on to the ways and means by

[1]See for example, C. Rose, *Sino-Japanese Relations: Facing the Past, Looking to the Future?* (London: Routledge, 2004); G. Rozman, *Northeast Asia's Stunted Regionalism: Bilateral Distrust in the Shadow of Globalization* (New York: Cambridge University Press, 2004); J. A. Fogel, *Articulating the Sinosphere: Sino-Japanese Relations in Space and Time* (Cambridge, MA: Harvard University Press, 2010); D. Lary, *The Chinese People at War* (New York: Cambridge University Press, 2010).

which China's rise is portrayed in South Korea. Since Korea's relations with *both* its more populous neighbors have been historically fraught, and since it is *also* implicated in various territorial disputes with both countries, determining Korean sensibilities is an important way of gaging shifts in public opinion across the region. How does the flare-up of a regional territorial dispute like Senkaku/Diaoyu — in which South Korea is not implicated — affect popular South Korean perceptions of China and Japan? Which side is more likely to be seen as a rival, and which side is framed as South Korea's friend as a result?

Employing a similar rationale and approach, we then explore how Japanese popular attitudes are framed in response to escalation in the disputes between South Korea and China over the Socotra Rock, which is submerged in the Yellow Sea, as well as the more conventionally *territorial* dispute over the Changbai/Paekdu mountain, which is actually situated between North Korea and China, but wholly claimed by both North and South Korea.[2]

Ultimately, our analysis of third-party popular perceptions in Northeast Asia will include analysis of Chinese opinions on tensions between South Korea and Japan over the Tokdo islets (known in Japan as Takeshima, and in the West as Liancourt Rocks), a dispute that has some parallels with Diaoyu/Senkaku. Preliminary investigations suggest that explicit connections between the Tokdo/Takeshima dispute and the Senkaku/Diaoyu one are rare in mainstream Chinese media and online.[3] This is symptomatic of the strong control exerted by the state on the media and cyberspace in China which complicates assessments of popular opinion on "sensitive issues". We limit our coverage of China here to a brief overview of online popular nationalism, before concentrating on the more comparable mediascapes

[2]For basic historic background and geographical features of the maritime and territorial disputes addressed here, see e.g., R. Guo, *Territorial Disputes and Resource Management: A Global Handbook* (New York: Nova Science, 2007).

[3]For example, there are no articles in the official *Renmin ribao* (*People's Daily*) that explicitly discuss the Tokdo and Diaoyu disputes in tandem. For an academic treatment, see M. Li and J. Qiu (2010). [South Korea's Effective Handling of the Tokdo Dispute Can Provide Lessons for China's Campaign to Protect its Sovereignty in Diaoyu], *Haiyang kaifa yu guanli*, 27.10.

and cyberspace ecologies of Japan and Korea that are the focus of this chapter.

The Popular Dynamics of Chinese Nationalism

When the Chinese Communist Party (CCP) began its patriotic education campaigns in the 1990s, nationalism was conceived as a reliable source of much needed legitimacy and popular support. However, the volatile nature of popular nationalism, particularly the virulent strain evident in Chinese cyberspace, has created unforeseen pressures for the government. The rise of popular nationalism has complicated the state's monopoly on foreign policy-making, for instance, by challenging the strategy of "hide and bide" through the 1990s and early 2000s, which was incompatible with the stridency of popular opinion.[4] Popular nationalism is thus a double-edged sword, both a source of legitimation for continued authoritarian rule, and "a means for the Chinese people to judge the performance of the state".[5] The party would prefer nationalism to be channelled and controlled like the regulated waters of a dam, but the strength of grassroots sentiments and the commercial imperatives that prevail in Chinese media and Chinese cyberspace make it difficult to turn on and off at will.[6] Furthermore, nationalism is not the sole prerogative of the state, and in many cases, it is led by commercial interests exploiting market demand: In the population at large and particularly in the comparatively free conditions that pertain in Chinese cyberspace, nationalism "sells". The world of online gaming provides an example of how state and commercial actors operate in cooperation to leverage popular demand. When the party accepted the

[4]For an example of the stridency of popular nationalism online, see Chase's analysis of Chinese reactions to UNESCO's decision to make the Goguryeo Tombs a world heritage site. T. Chase (2011). "Nationalism and the Net: Online Discussion of Goguryeo History in China and South Korea", *China Information*, 25.1: 61–82.

[5]S. Zhao (2013). "Foreign Policy Implications of Chinese Nationalism Revisited: The Strident Turn", *Journal of Contemporary China*, 22.82: 535–553.

[6]D. Stockmann (2011). "Race to the Bottom: Media Marketization and Increasing Negativity Toward the United States in China", *Political Communication*, 28.3: 268–290; Y. Jiang, *Cyber-Nationalism in China: Challenging Western Media Portrayals of Internet Censorship* (Adelaide: University of Adelaide Press, 2012).

popularity of gaming, particularly among the younger population, it seized on it as a pedagogical opportunity. Online games were declared "cultural products" and the state made substantial investments in the industry so that "patriotic online games became a joint enterprise between the Party-state and private companies".[7] In combination, state and commercial interests were highly effective in inculcating popular nationalist sentiments, through online games like the War of Resistance series where players take on the role of various Chinese forces fighting against the Japanese occupiers in various bloody scenarios. Such games appear to be particularly popular among the "angry youth" (*fenqing* 愤青) that constitute one of the most stridently nationalistic cohorts. This demographic is also especially connected and active online,[8] responsible for much of the mobilization that periodically spills over into physical world demonstrations.

Yet, despite the rapid growth of the Chinese internet population and fast-moving social media, the state has demonstrated the continuing capacity to contain popular nationalism. As Jessica Weiss shows in her analysis of state management of anti-foreign protests from 1985 to 2012, where prevailing diplomatic conditions and strategic context demands it, the state is able and willing to control anti-Japanese demonstrations, both in the physical world where its capacities are not in doubt, and online.[9] The information order in cyberspace is facilitated by multiple layers of monitoring and control, reinforced by a sophisticated censorship regime and propaganda mechanisms. State control of the physical infrastructure of the internet and a binding legal framework creates a norm of self-censorship and self-regulation that ensures that commercial internet companies do not act against the state's regularly updated strategic objectives. Thus, as Beijing sought to improve relations with Tokyo from 2006 to 2010, activities of online petitions and mobilization of offline demonstrations were regularly and robustly restricted. The scale of this resolve was demonstrated on the eve

---

[7]H. Nie (2013). "Gaming, Nationalism, and Ideological Work in Contemporary China: Online Games Based on the War of Resistance Against Japan", *Journal of Contemporary China*, 22.81: 499–517.

[8]J. Sullivan (2014). "China's Weibo: Is Faster Different?" *New Media & Society*, 16.1: 24–37.

[9]J. Weiss, *Powerful Patriots: Nationalist Protest in China's Foreign Relations* (Oxford: Oxford University Press, 2014).

of a sensitive anniversary in Sino-Japan relations, when efforts in Chinese cyberspace to organize offline demonstrations were so tightly restricted that the Chinese term "Diaoyu" was blocked, while "Senkaku" evaded censorship.[10] On other occasions, notably Japan's bid for a permanent seat on the UN Security Council in 2005 and nationalization of the disputed islands in 2012, online and offline protests have been allowed to proceed.

Comparing anti-Japan protests over two decades, Reilly describes a cyclical pattern in which "a single inflammatory event can spread rapidly across a broad segment of the engaged public, stimulating online debates and activism that can spill over into the streets".[11] Although such grassroots mobilization may initially be tolerated by the state, and encouraged by commercial incentives related to a receptive public, the state's cost-benefit calculation changes over time. At the point that the state calculates that demonstrations may start to jeopardize domestic stability, long-term foreign policy objectives, trade relations, etc., the state's information control regime is engaged, controlling the tone of media coverage, censoring discussion, and putting out counter-narratives.[12] Numerous scholars have noted how online and physical world protests can be useful in terms of a safety valve allowing people to blow off steam, as a feedback mechanism alerting authorities to how strongly the public feels about an issue, a tool in internal power competitions, in terms of signaling behavior.[13] However, scholars have also identified how protests can spiral out of control, as was the case with the 1999 US Embassy protests following the NATO bombing of the Chinese Embassy bombing in Belgrade. Nationalist causes can also

[10]H. Han, "Protect the—[Unacceptable Input]", September 12, 2010, in A. Barr (trans./ed.), *This Generation: Dispatches from China's Most Popular Blogger* (London: Simon Schuster, 2010), pp. 182–184.

[11]J. Reilly (2014). "A Wave to Worry About? Public Opinion, Foreign Policy and China's Anti-Japan Protests", *Journal of Contemporary China*, 23.86: 197–215.

[12]J. Reilly, *Strong Society, Smart State: The Rise of Public Opinion in China's Japan Policy* (New York: Columbia University Press, 2012).

[13]J. Hasid (2012). "Safety Valve or Pressure Cooker? Blogs in Chinese Political Life", *Journal of Communication*, 62.2: 212–230; J. Sullivan (2012). "A Tale of Two Microblogs in China", *Media, Culture & Society*, 34.6: 773–783; S. Shen and S. Breslin (eds.), *Online Chinese Nationalism and Chinese Bilateral Relations* (Lanham, MD: Rowman and Littlefield, 2010); J. Weiss (2013). "Authoritarian Signalling, Mass Audiences and Nationalist Protest in China", *International Organization*, 67.1: 1–35.

mutate, with anger being redirected against the state. Goubin Yang observes that, "as online protests against Japan indicate, online nationalist protests may open up new spaces for citizens to exert their discursive rights".[14] In other cases, like the protests against atrocities committed against ethnic Chinese in Indonesia in 1998, the state has been attacked for demonstrating insufficient patriotism.[15]

Korean Attitudes: Suspicion/Fear of China and Resentment toward Japan

The Korean peninsula has historically been exposed to multiple interventions from both China and Japan. China's involvement in Korean affairs began very early during the time of the Han dynasty (206 BC–220 AD). The Chinese invaded the proto-Korean kingdom of Gojoseon during the reign of Han Wudi and established four commanderies in what is now North Korea in 108 BC. Since then, the Chinese have periodically intervened both diplomatically and militarily in Korean internal affairs, the latest example being the Chinese military aid given to North Korea during the Korean War (1950–1953).[16] Similarly, the Japanese continuously troubled Korea's southern border regions with their infamous Waegu/Wokou pirate raids and full-scale invasions (Toyotomi Hideyoshi's invasions (1592–1598) and the Japanese occupation and colonization of Korea (1910–1945)).[17] This long history of being on the receiving end of Chinese or Japanese military aggression has left a deep, innate, and ever-present feeling of grievance among many Koreans toward their two powerful neighbors.

---

[14] G. Yang, *The Power of the Internet in China: Citizen Activism Online* (New York: Columbia University Press, 2009), p. 56.

[15] C. Hughes (2000). "Nationalism in Chinese Cyberspace", *Cambridge Review of International Affairs*, 13.2: 195–209.

[16] For a full history of China's involvement in the Korean War, see J. Chen, *China's Road to the Korean War: The Making of the Sino-American Confrontation* (New York: Columbia University Press, 1994), and S. G. Zhang, *Mao's Military Romanticism: China and the Korean War, 1950–1953* (Lawrence, KS: University Press of Kansas, 1995).

[17] For a detailed analysis of Japanese imperialism and aggression toward Korea and the rest of East Asia, see W. G. Beasley, *Japanese Imperialism 1894–1945* (Oxford: Oxford University Press, 1991).

Some Koreans fear China's rising power and are suspicious of its intentions toward Korea. At the same time, they feel resentment toward Japan, which brutally colonized Korea in the early 20th century (1910–1945) and still offend Koreans regularly with historical revisionism (the comfort women issue in particular[18]) and territorial claims to Tokdo which the Japanese call Takeshima.[19] Tokdo and Comfort Women are emotive issues that regularly inflame nationalist sentiments in Korea and although they have little potential to cause a real military conflict between Korea and Japan, they have contributed significantly to the formation of pro-Chinese opinion among some segments of the Korean public in the case of the Senkaku/Diaoyu Islands dispute.

While it is highly likely that Japan is still viewed more negatively in Korea than China, at least among the general public, among the academic and policy-making elite, China is now much more of a source of fear and suspicion. This fear that was already apparent due to Communist China's military intervention and invasion of South Korea during the Korean War (1950–1953, in support of the Kim dynasty in North Korea and in opposition to the US and South Korea), was re-ignited in all sectors of Korean society, not just among the elite, because of the so-called Northeast Project, 동북공정. The revisionist Chinese claims to what the Korean public regards as historical Korean states such as Goguryeo and Balhae (동북공정),[20] has over the past decade sparked an emotional response among nationalistic Koreans and heightened anti-Chinese sentiment in Korea.

[18]See S. Schellstede Choi, *Comfort Women Speak: Testimony by Sex Slaves of the Japanese Military* (New York: Holmes and Meier, 2000).

[19]There is an immense amount of literature on this dispute in Korean and in other languages. However, they cannot be discussed here. Needless to say this territorial dispute, which South Korea refuses to even acknowledge as a dispute officially, since Tokdo is *de jure* and *de facto* part of Korea, continues to poison Korea–Japan relations.

[20]This highly publicized and acrimonious dispute between China and Korea over ancient history is also mirrored by an equally acrimonious disagreement over more recent history between Korea and Japan which receives treatment in K. Kimijima, "The Continuing Legacy of Japanese Colonialism: The Japan–South Korea Joint Study Group on History Textbooks", in L. Hein and M. Selden (eds.), *Censoring History: Citizenship and Memory in Japan, Germany, and the United States* (Armonk, NY: M.E. Sharpe, 2000), pp. 203–225.

The claims to Goguryeo (also known as Koguryo) and Balhae are part of China's concerted effort to strengthen its historical–territorial claims[21] on its borders and also to allay its own internal security concerns.[22] This assertiveness has offended the vast majority of the South Korean public.[23]

As a corollary to this renewed anti-Chinese sentiment, one of the best-known narratives of Korea's historic struggle against China, the wars fought by Goguryeo in the 7th century against the Sui dynasty (589–618 AD) and then subsequently the powerful Tang dynasty (618–907 AD), have been re-emphasized to highlight Korean resistance to Chinese aggression. This is reflected by the immense popularity of historical dramas such as KBS's Dae Jo Yeong (2006–2007) that glorified Goguryeo's heroic resistance to Tang China and was produced with the deliberate aim of countering China's historical revisionism.[24] A reflection of the equally, if not more, virulent anti-Japanese sentiment in Korea is given by the success of KBS's historical drama KBS Immortal Yi Sun Shin, that celebrated the life of

[21]These claims are in turn buttressed by the growing nationalist sentiments of the Chinese people. For Chinese nationalism, see J. Townsend, "Chinese Nationalism", in J. Unger (ed.), *Chinese Nationalism* (Armonk, NY: M.E. Sharpe, 1996), pp. 1–30, especially p. 17 ff, and P. Duara, "De-constructing the Chinese Nation", in J. Unger (ed.), *Chinese Nationalism* (Armonk, NY: M.E. Sharpe, 1996), pp. 31–55. See also W. Zheng, *Never Forget National Humiliation: Historical Memory in Chinese Politics and Foreign Relations* (New York: Columbia University Press, 2012). For a critique of the pseudo-historical approach adopted to legitimize modern territorial claims, see Q. E. Wang, *Inventing China through History: The May Fourth Approach to Historiography* (Albany, NY: State University of New York Press, 2001), p. 121. See also K. C. Chang (2001). "Reflections on Chinese Archaeology in the Second Half of the Twentieth Century", *Journal of East Asian Archaeology*, 3.1–3.12: 5–13.

[22]For detailed analyses of this dispute over Goguryeo (Koguryo) and its significance, see P. Hays Gries (2005). "The Koguryo Controversy, National Identity, and Sino-Korean Relations Today", *East Asia*, 22.4: 3–17, and D. Chen (2012). "Domestic Politics, National Identity, and International Conflict: The Case of the Koguryo Controversy", *Journal of Contemporary China*, 21.74: 227–241. See also http://www.japanfocus.org/-Andrei-Lankov/2233 and http://www.japanfocus.org/-Yonson-Ahn/2631 for further discussion.

[23]For excellent analyses of the dispute over ancient history between China and South Korea and the negative effects of nationalist indoctrination in both countries, see S. S. Yi, *Created Antiquity: The Early Modern Nation-State's Story of East Asia* (Seoul: Samin, 2001), pp. 19–34, 186–88; J. O. Yi, *The History of Goguryeo* (Seoul: Gimyoungsa, 2005), pp. 12–23.

[24]See http://www.kbs.co.kr/drama/daejoyoung/about/plan/index.html.

Korea's foremost military hero, the admiral Yi Sun Shin, who defended Korea against Japanese invaders in the 16th century.

Many in South Korea, especially the policy planning elite, fear that China's historical revisionism (the so-called "Northeast Project") is merely a smokescreen designed to establish historical claims to territory in North Korea in the same way that Chinese Emperor Tang Taizong (r. CE 626–649) used "history" to justify Tang occupation of Goguryeo territory.[25] For instance, Bak Changhee of Gukbang University argues that China has traditionally viewed the Korean peninsula as its sphere of influence and will intervene to protect what it sees as its vested interests in North Korea.[26] He also asserts that China's ultimate strategic goal is to expand its power further into the Korean peninsula, separate South Korea from its alliance with the US, and establish a pro-Chinese government in the whole of the peninsula.[27] Such fears of Chinese aggression must be taken into consideration when we examine Korean attitudes, especially academic attitudes toward the islands dispute between China and Japan.

Chinese support for North Korea and perceived snub of South Korea following the sinking of the South Korean warship Cheonan in 2010, have only heightened such fears. Yi Sanghyun from the ministry of foreign affairs argues that China's rise and continued support for North Korea's Kim dynasty represents a potential threat to South Korea's security, that China's ambition is to turn Korea into a buffer zone and dominate the East China Sea (excluding other powers such as the USA from east Asian waters), and that China's so-called "peaceful rise" might not be so peaceful after all.[28] He also asserts that China's recent behavior toward Korea conceals a desire to view Sino-Korean relations in the light of the tributary relations

---

[25] B. R. Shin, "The Perspective of Tang Taizong towards the Three Eastern Kingdoms: Searching for the origins of the Northeast Project", in J. S. Lee and S. H. Jo (eds.), *Conflict in the Korean Peninsula and China's Intervention* (Seoul: Sunin, 2012), pp. 17–49, esp. pp. 19 and 49.

[26] C. H. Park, "Crisis in North Korea and China's Military Intervention", in J. S. Lee and S. H. Jo (eds.), *Conflict in the Korean Peninsula and China's Intervention* (Seoul: Sunin, 2012), pp. 221–251.

[27] C. H. Park (2012), pp. 225 and 228.

[28] S. H. Yi, "The Rise of China and the Response of the US: Security Implications for Korea", in J. S. Lee and S. H. Jo (eds.), *Conflict in the Korean Peninsula and China's Intervention* (Seoul: Sunin, 2012), pp. 253–286.

that existed between Korea and China in the pre-modern, "feudal" era, i.e., that it is an expression of arrogance. A fear of Chinese maritime expansion and ambitions toward Ieodo (이어도) and Korea's Exclusive Economic Zones (EEZs) in the East China Sea has also been raised by academics engaged in Korean naval defense planning. Cha Do Hee for instance emphasizes the fact that the US and China are engaged in a power struggle over naval hegemony in East Asia and that in order to defend Korea's maritime borders, trade routes and economic interests in the East China Sea (which includes the disputed islands of Senkaku/Diaoyu), a strengthening of the US–Korea military alliance, and the expansion of Korean naval capacity are needed to counter China's growing expansionist ambitions.[29]

The Senkaku/Diaoyu Islands Dispute in Korean Media and Blogs

The territorial dispute between Japan and China over the Senkaku/Diaoyu Islands has been followed with keen interest by the South Korean media, bloggers, and international relations experts, primarily because its peaceful resolution or violent implosion may have significant ramifications for possible future handlings by South Korea of its own territorial disputes with both Japan (Tokdo dispute) and China (Ieodo, Baekdusan, and the Gando disputes). Korean attitudes concerning the dispute between China and Japan are very diverse ranging from those who express sympathy for China (usually those among the general public whose political sympathies are left-aligned or have strong anti-Japanese sentiments) to those who vouch for careful, guarded neutrality or advocate anti-Chinese and pro-Japanese policies (usually those who are on the right wing of the political spectrum and are hostile to China's perceived territorial ambitions in East Asia). These differing opinions and attitudes among Koreans are inseparably linked to

[29]D. H. Cha, *The US–China Rivalry Over Naval Hegemony in East Asia: The Transfer of Naval Power between the US and China with a Special Focus on Attack on the Cheonanham* (Seoul: Book Korea, 2012), pp. 253–290. Similar concerns regarding the challenge presented by China's maritime ambitions and its effect on the security of Korea's own maritime interests and trade routes can be found in J. H. Yi, *China's Maritime Strategy* (Seoul: Gold Egg, 2007), pp. 238–242.

Korea's historical relations with both countries, memories of which can still inflame nationalist sentiments within Korea. These historical memories of past grievances (directed at both Japan and China, but more so at Japan) when coupled with existing territorial disputes and economic and strategic concerns produce a very complex and varied reaction among the Korean public and academic community. All these aspects of the Korean reaction to and representation of the disputes between China and Japan will be explored below.

As noted earlier, the majority of the Korean policy planning elite and international relations experts (who generally tend to be more conservative than the mass media and netizens) are more concerned about the present threat/pressure coming from China than about past historical grievances toward Japan. Many are of the opinion that Korea should, while maintaining a show of neutrality to avoid antagonizing China, give support to the maintenance of the status quo with Japan in possession of the disputed islands, since an outright Chinese victory in the affair would lead to the domination by China of the vital sea lanes through which the majority of Korea's trade traffic and energy supplies pass through.[30]

However, the anti-Japanese sentiments generated by Japan's repeatedly provocative behavior with regard to the Comfort Women issue and also the continuing Tokdo dispute with Japan made outright support for Japan in 2012 a very unappealing course of action for the Korean public in general.[31] The Korean media and internet bloggers repeatedly pointed out Japan's

---

[30]The more radical exponent of this view is H. B. Gang, *China's Surprise Attack: The Three Way Struggle between Korea, China and Japan with a Focus on the Ryukyu Islands* (Seoul: Human & Books, 2012). However, there is a general wariness among the policy planning elite of South Korea about China's naval expansion in the East and South China Seas, which they feel can develop into a long-term threat to Korea's economic and strategic interests. A strengthening of the alliance and cooperation with the US and Japan as a means of countering Chinese naval expansion is the dominant thinking among policy planners in Seoul. See C. H. Jeong, *The East Asian Naval Strategy of the US and China and Korea's Maritime Security: The Effect of the Competition and Struggle between the US and China over Control of the South China Sea* (Seongnam: Sejong Yeonguso, 2012), p. 64.

[31]Anti-Japanese sentiment generated by yet another spat with Japan over Tokdo in 2012 shortly before the dispute over the Senkakus/Diaoyu flared up again between China and Japan, influenced the views of the South Korean mass media and also bloggers toward the dispute between China and Japan.

hypocrisy in claiming territory currently controlled by Korea, yet denying China's historical claims to territory controlled by Japan. In other words, they suggested that Japan's position vis-à-vis China is similar to Korea's position in relation to Japan. This was often accompanied by the hope that the resolution of the Senkaku/Diaoyu Islands dispute would be peaceful and yield useful precedents for Korea to utilize in its own territorial dispute with Japan.[32] Most of the Korean media[33] and bloggers[34] eventually adopted a semi-neutral stance, taking jibes at the Japanese for their double standards when it comes to territorial disputes, but not supporting China either since Korea is comfortable with neither China nor Japan. Policy planners and academics in general advocated a careful, measured response to the dispute between Japan and China while making sure to pick up any developments that might bc of use in future negotiations with China and Japan over Korea's territorial disputes with both powers.

However, political divisions within Korea meant that there was as usual a pro-Chinese minority that attempted to utilize the anti-Japanese feeling in Korea and resulting sympathy, albeit brief, for China among the Korean public (as mentioned above largely due to anger toward Japan over Tokdo), to generally advance China's interests, which they view as matching their own political goals, that of advancing rapprochement with North Korea with

[32]For instance, http://blog.daum.net/jongropjk/801138; http://blog.naver.com/cusecret?Redirect=Log&logNo=80181534469; http://blog.naver.com/msnayana?Redirect=Log&logNo=80178405363. The reader commentaries/responses to this blog's neutral approach and call for moderation were positive with all commentaries emphasizing the negative economic consequences for Korea should the situation escalate.

[33]Every South Korean newspaper entry/editorial on the Senkaku–Diaoyu Islands dispute prior to September 26, 2013 has been accessed and analyzed for the purposes of this chapter.

[34]Similarly, every Korean blog which discussed the crisis prior to September 26, 2013 have been accessed and analyzed. Unfortunately, there is simply no way of quantifying the extent to which these blogs and newspaper entries reflect Korean public opinion, since no polls were taken to determine accurately how the general public view the crisis and the belligerents involved. If, however, the representation in mass media (in this case, newspapers and blogs) is taken as a reflection of the way in which the situation is presented to the Korean general public, their overall impact on public opinion is quite apparent. Therefore, a comprehensive analysis of these blogs, reader commentaries, and newspapers is a useful exercise in assessing public opinion in the absence of concrete polling data.

Chinese aid and moving Korea out of America's sphere of influence.[35] The left-aligned newspapers, bloggers, and netizens in Korea, who traditionally favored Communist China and appeasement of North Korea, therefore represented the islands dispute in a decidedly pro-Chinese light, casting the Japanese as imperialists who had stolen Chinese territory just as they now seek to steal Korean territory.[36]

Ohmy News, a radical left-wing newspaper, emphasized that Japan stole the islands from China while China was weak in the 19th century and then held on to them with US aid.[37] *Hankyoreh* (한겨레신문), another left-wing newspaper published an article titled "Are the Diaoyu Islands becoming the second Manchuria", hinting thereby that Japanese occupation of the islands is as illegal as had been the Japanese takeover of Manchuria in the 1930s, thereby faithfully repeating the views of PRC Chinese newspapers on the issue.[38] Similarly, left-wing bloggers openly claimed that the islands belong to China and that the only reason that Japan can indulge in disputing ownership of Tokdo and the Diaoyu Islands with both Korea and China simultaneously is because of American "imperialist" support. Thus, while fanning anti-Japanese sentiments, they also sought to trigger anti-American sentiments as well, while putting a gloss of neutrality on their views by advocating that Korea do nothing in support of either parties, clearly a message directed at refuting the views of conservatives who sought more active cooperation with Japan and the US against China in the East China Sea.[39]

More right-wing newspapers have in contrast shown ambiguous attitudes toward the dispute. The right-wing daily *Dong-A Ilbo* loudly denounced Japan's militarist past as part of the denunciation of Japan's territorial claims on Tokdo and historical revisionism on the Comfort

---

[35] J. G. Gang and G. H. Park (2012). *The Road to Peace for the Korean Peninsula in the G2 Era*, Pyonghwa-Tongil Yeonguso (Research Institute for Peaceful Unification) (Seoul: Hanul, 2012), pp. 64–66, 73, 419.

[36] See http://jgh712.blog.me/167919034.

[37] See http://www.ohmynews.com/NWS Web/View/at_pg.aspx?CNTN_CD=A000178 1900.

[38] See http://www.hani.co.kr/arti/international/china/553949.html.

[39] See http://jgh712.blog.me/167919034.

Women issue.[40] However, with regard to the islands dispute, it was more concerned about the economic fallout from the Sino-Japanese conflict than about the issue of who deserves Korea's support.[41] The conservative *Chosunilbo* also vocally denounced Japanese aggression on the Tokdo issue and warned that if Japan continues to veer to the far right, it will fall into ruin as it did during the Second World War. It added further that Japan's actions with regard to the Tokdo and Senkaku Islands disputes show that Japan is still dreaming the delusional militaristic vision of expansion that brought Japan low in the past.[42] However, the paper also soon balanced this sharp rebuke of Japan with caution about supporting China on the issue. The paper reminds viewers that the Chinese claims in the East China Sea and the Seas off the coasts of Okinawa already may infringe of the territorial rights and economic interests of Korea to the south.[43]

The *Joongangilbo*, another conservative daily, went as far as to claim that Japan's lurch to right is reaching dangerous levels and that Japan is on its way to developing a nuclear weapons program that is threatening to Korea.[44] However, in blogs associated with the paper, China was also vehemently denounced for its arrogant attitude and territorial ambitions in the East China Sea, the ultimate goal of which, it was claimed, is to create a new tributary system in its favor in East Asia.[45] Other conservative or center-right newspapers tended to emphasize more the fact that this territorial dispute between China and Japan has the potential to also infringe on Korea's territorial claims and EEZs in the south sea.[46]

Because of the similarities between this dispute and the Tokdo dispute between Korea and Japan, the Korean blogosphere has featured some

---

[40] See http://news.donga.com/3/all/20121128/51163033/1 and http://shindonga.donga.com/docs/magazine/shin/2012/09/21/201209210500022/201209210500022_1.html.

[41] See http://economy.donga.com/3/all/20121018/50201463/1 and http://economy.donga.com/3/all/20120919/49519494/1.

[42] See http://forum.chosun.com/bbs.message.view.screen?bbs_id=1010&message_id=1000985.

[43] See http://news.chosun.com/site/data/html_dir/2012/12/23/2012122300827.html.

[44] See http://magazine.joinsmsn.com/monthly/article_view.asp?aid=293745.

[45] See http://blog.joinsmsn.com/media/folderListSlide.asp?uid=woodyhan&folder=1&list_id=12101012.

[46] See http://www.hankyung.com/news/app/newsview.php?aid=2012122776018&intype=1.

interesting commentaries on the issue. Although it is difficult to quantify, at the outbreak of the crisis in 2012, the dominant response to the dispute among Korean netizens who left comments on blogs and newspapers online was support for China and hatred for Japan that was disputing Tokdo with Korea. However, by the time bloggers started analyzing the situation in detail, the mood had palpably shifted somewhat. Some blogs placed the dispute within the context of other territorial disputes across East Asia mostly involving China and also Japan, and adopted a dispassionate commentary approach.[47] Some were even surprisingly hostile to China and accused the Chinese government of using the issue to hide internal problems and also justify its naval build-up which is a threat to Korea.[48]

Still others advocated caution and warned against openly supporting China on the issue, despite dislike of Japan, because Korea's position vis-à-vis Japan on Tokdo is actually more similar to Japan's vis-à-vis China, than China's vis-à-vis Japan. If Japan were to lose the Senkakus on grounds proposed by China, Korea may be placed at a disadvantage, if disputes escalated over Tokdo with Japan, on those same grounds. Also people were reminded that Korea also has ongoing territorial disputes with China as well.[49] Many were simply neutral on the issue, noting the huge economic and strategic benefits of controlling these islands which is driving both China and Japan to contest them, and advised that Koreans simply be observant about the arguments employed by both sides in advancing their claims.[50] Some were however more emotive and expressed a common feeling of sorts with the Chinese because of Korea's problem with Japan on the Tokdo issue and advocated support for China on the issue.[51]

---

[47] See http://blog.naver.com/xuanxie?Redirect=Log&logNo=40158570079; http://blog.naver.com/contentsy?Redirect=Log&logNo=60176001033.

[48] See http://yum0927.blog.me/10147969156.

[49] See http://newstar3.blog.me/120169444539.

[50] See http://politicstory.tistory.com/681; http://blog.naver.com/rj2222?Redirect=Log&logNo=50159012831; http://blog.naver.com/maenam111?Redirect=Log&logNo=90153451160; http://caihongblog.com/130146993539.

[51] See http://blog.naver.com/psy504244?Redirect=Log&logNo=10150830058; http://blog.naver.com/maenam111?Redirect=Log&logNo=90150446238; http://blog.naver.com/ohyak?Redirect=Log&logNo=50150423170; http://blog.naver.com/touchchina?Redirect=Log&logNo=20172811669; http://blog.daum.net/hoongoni/44; http://blog.naver.com/maenam111?Redirect=Log&logNo=90164331209.

As time passed and disputes with China returned to the attention of Koreans, the initial warmth of Korean feeling toward China, which was perceived to be engaged in the same struggle as Korea against the aggressions of Japan, slowly but surely cooled and the majority of newspaper editorials and blogs (including reader commentaries) swung in the direction of caution and the urge to pick sides in the dispute quickly vanished. The advice of most bloggers and academic experts was to keep a level head, be alert about what the dispute will mean for Korea, and to think strategically for the national benefit. Korea as usual stuck in the middle between Japan and China has its share of pro-Japanese (less vocal) and pro-Chinese (more vocal) advocates. However, the vast majority in the middle seem now to favor a much more nuanced and sensible approach to the dispute, which is in line with the caution displayed by the rest of the international community on the issue.

Socotra Rock: A Sino-Korean Bone of Contention

The dispute between China and South Korea over the Socotra Rock involves complex historical, nationalistic, territorial, administrative, economic, and defense issues. Interestingly, Socotra Rock remains relatively unknown to the outside world — including Japan. Indeed, one Japanese netizen has frankly admitted that Socotra Rock is "unfamiliar to [Japanese] ears".[52] This perhaps necessitates a brief introduction. Socotra Rock (lat. 125° 10′56.81″E; long. 32°07′22.63″N) is located in the Yellow Sea, laying some 150 km southwest from South Korea's Marado Island, and some 250 km northeast from China's Haijiao Island (the nearest Japanese island is located only 275 km away). Known in Korean as Ieodo (or Parangdo) and in Chinese as Suyan, it is not an island but a submerged coral reef which, at low tide, is 4.6 m beneath the ocean's surface. Centuries-old Korean legends caution that sailors and fishermen who see the reef will never return home; the British merchant vessel, *Socotra*, which spotted the reef in 1900 (and which presumably remained ignorant of Korean legends) not only returned to London but also bestowed upon the reef its English-language name, Socotra Rock.

[52]"Tsui ni Chūgoku to Kankoku ga Sendo Funsō e!" *News US*, September 26, 2012. Available at: http://www.news-us.jp/article/294146034.html.

Japan's victory in the Russo-Japanese War in 1904–1905 ensured, over the ensuing decades, that the Imperial Japanese Navy maintained control of the waters surrounding Socotra Rock. This remained the case until Japan's defeat in World War II. Thereafter, Socotra Rock bubbled beneath the surface of Sino-South Korean relations. In 1952, even as the Korean War raged, the South Korean government promulgated the so-called Syngman Rhee line. This line specifically included Socotra Rock within Korean territorial waters. The People's Republic of China declined to recognize this line. South Korea in the 1990s ignored Chinese objections and began building a weather station on Socotra Rock.

Not until completion of the weather station did Socotra Rock become a hot-button issue in Sino-South Korean relations. Technically speaking, the dispute is not a territorial issue. According to the United Nations Convention on the Law of the Sea, a submerged reef — such as Socotra Rock — cannot be considered national territory. Yet, in seemingly open defiance of the UN, the South Korean government insists that "Socotra Rock is clearly South Korean territory". At the very least, South Korea maintains that it will not budge from the basic insistence that Socotra Rock falls within its own EEZ. The Chinese government, which also claims that Socotra Rock lies within its own EEZ, has registered its "opposition" to "unilateral [South Korean] actions" on Socotra Rock.[53] In March 2012, a Chinese official hinted at Chinese unilateralism concerning Socotra Rock. The official sparked a diplomatic row when he publicly noted that, because Socotra Rock is located in Chinese waters, it is most certainly Chinese.

It is difficult to characterize Japanese responses to this Sino-South Korea diplomatic row. Some have expressed surprise. "Territorial disputes are not only a Sino-Japanese and Korean–Japanese issue", commented the online news source, *News US*.[54] The vastly more reputable *Newsweek* carried an article with a similar sentiment; it noted that China's seemingly

[53]S. Kijirō (2007). "Chūgoku no Tōhoku Kōtei to Chōsenshi Shinryaku to Kita Chōsen" [China's Northeastern Process, Invasion in Korean History, and North Korea], *Yamaguchi Keizaigaku Zasshi* [*Yamaguchi Economics Journal*], 55(5): 135–137.

[54]"Tsui ni Chūgoku to Kankoku ga Sendo Funsō e!", *News US*, September 26, 2012. Available at: http://www.news-us.jp/article/294146034.html.

"endless" appetite encompassed "not just Okinawa".[55] Such surprise is perhaps understandable. On the one hand, Socotra Rock (as already noted) remains largely unknown in Japan. On the other hand, the Japanese are preoccupied with their own nation's manifold territorial disputes, including those involving not only China and South Korea but also Russia, North Korea, and Taiwan.

Some Japanese see in the Socotra Rock dispute confirmation of what they regard as Chinese expansionism. The above-mentioned *News US* put it simply: "China's plan to conquer East Asia has at last begun to gain momentum".[56] One netizen voiced a similar notion: "China is showing its limitless greed".[57] One blogger reckoned that, because the colonial powers (including Japan) had sliced China up in the 19th and early 20th centuries, China now "wants to expand its defensive line as far as possible". That defensive line, according to this blogger, extends far beyond the Asian mainland and most certainly includes Socotra Rock, principally because the Chinese want to fight the United States in the Pacific.[58]

Japanese bloggers do not spare South Korea in their analysis of the dispute over Socotra Rock. At least one blogger has pointed to the discrepancy between the South Korean *territorial* claim over Socotra Rock and the UN's insistence that a sunken reef cannot be national territory.[59] Another pointed to the South Korean government's express desire for "sincere" discussions with China — and questioned then President Lee Myung-bak's own sincerity. As evidence, this blogger pointed to Lee's rejection of then Japanese Prime Minister Noda Yoshihiko's letter concerning the Liancourt

---

[55] "Okinawa dake ja nai, Chūgoku no Hatenaki Sendo Ego" [It's not just Okinawa, China's infinite territorial ego], *Newsweek Japan*, January 21, 2013. Available at: http://www.newsweekjapan.jp/stories/world/2013/05/post-2923.php.

[56] "Tsui ni Chūgoku to Kankoku ga Sendo Funsō e!", *News US*, September 26, 2012. Available at: http://www.news-us.jp/article/294146034.html.

[57] "Ima, Wadai no Nyuzu o Otodoke Shimasu", September 25, 2012. Available at: http://hottrendhotnews.blog.so-net.ne.jp/2012-09-25.

[58] "Debuo Nikki", February 17, 2010. Available at: http://debuo02.seesaa.net/article/141218042.html.

[59] "Hatena Diary", November 9, 2012. Available at: http://d.hatena.ne.jp/warabidani/20121109/p2.

Rocks.[60] It should also be acknowledged that Japan's fringe-dwelling extreme right-wing takes delight in the Sino-South Korean dispute over Socotra Rock; the extreme right tends to be derisive in its treatment of South Korea. One example should suffice: China is "conscious that it is lying" about its claim over Socotra Rock, while South Korea is a "paranoid, compulsive liar". The blog concludes by noting that, if China continues to insist that even Okinawa Prefecture is Chinese territory, then Korea's fate is all but sealed. It predicts the arrival of the day when the Korean peninsula again becomes a Chinese "tributary".[61]

One armchair strategist believes that Japan and South Korea could "clash" militarily over the Takeshima/Tokdo and that such a Japanese–South Korean clash would provide China with a "good opportunity to attack and occupy Socotra Rock". Our erstwhile armchair strategist noted that South Korea would then find itself fighting great powers on either side, and concluded that Poland's fate at the hands of Germany and the Soviet Union in 1939 could well revisit South Korea. Such thinking sparked comments from any number of other armchair strategists. "Has China realized that is not in its best interests to go to war with Japan?" asked one. Another lamented the Japanese government's unwillingness to take a similarly "hard-line stance" in its dealings with its neighbors.[62]

There are also those who would welcome Japan's active involvement in the dispute over Socotra Rock. The Rock evidently lies within Japan's Air Defense Identification Zone (ADIZ), which at the very least, means that planes flying thereover must first gain Japan's approval. This includes the South Korean Air Force; one self-proclaimed expert in Japanese–Korean relations wrote in October 2012 that the South Korean Air Force had sought and received Japan's permission to fly over Socotra Rock 17 times that year.[63] Some bloggers emerged convinced that Socotra

[60] "Okinawa no Ama no jaku no Kansō", September 27, 2012. Available at: http://blogs.yahoo.co.jp/okiwindom/folder/950683.html?m=lc&p=6.
[61] "Toraneko Nikki", September 30, 2012. Available at: http://ryotaroneko.ti-da.net/d2012-09-30.html.
[62] "Kokusai Jōsei no Bunseki to Yoso", September 14, 2012. Available at: http://blog.goo.ne.jp/princeofwales1941/e/10258bf3b5a4a2922d6131994142538a?newwindow=true.
[63] "Shinshiari no Burogu", October 5, 2010. Available at: http://ameblo.jp/sincerelee/entry-11372285563.html.

Rock is indeed "Japanese territory". Almost invariably, this sparked the imaginations of the internet's wannabe diplomats. "If you swap Takeshima", wrote one, "Japan will recognize [South Korea's claim to Socotra Rock]".[64]

The Changbai/Paekdu Dispute through Japanese Eyes

Japanese perceptions of the Sino-Korean dispute over Changbai/Paekdu Mountain are equally fragmented and complex. Changbai/Paekdu Mountain's volcanic summit cups a crater lake on the Sino-North Korean border. Chinese regard Changbai (Chinese name) Mountain as very much part of Manchuria; Koreans see Paekdu (Korean name) Mountain as the birthplace of their culture and also remember it as the nerve center of resistance to Japan's colonial rule over their peninsula during the early 20th century. North Korean leader Kim Jong-il was, moreover, (reputedly) born on Changbai/Paekdu Mountain, and the North Korean government regards it as "sacred territory".[65]

Let us begin with a survey — however brief — of academic views of the dispute. Akizuki Nozomi has argued that the Changbai/Paekdu issue (like other territorial issues in the region) has arisen at least partly because of the difficulties inherent in applying modern international law to areas which until the 1800s operated under a very different world system. Akizuki has also reminded readers that Japan sought definitive answers to territorial questions in the early 20th century. In this regard, he has drawn readers' attention to Shinoda Jisaku's ground-breaking 1938 study of the Sino-Korean border, which asserted unequivocally that Changbai/Paekdu Mountain had long been Korean territory.[66] Kyoto University's Nakanishi Terumasa has recently written of a "new Cold War"

---

[64] "Desukutoppu 2 Channeru", October 6, 2012. Available at: http://desktop2ch.tv/news4plus/1349515067/.

[65] Kim Ki-chan, *Kuhaku no Kita Chosen Gendaishi: Pekutosan o Utta Kim Il-sung* (Tokyo: Shinchosha, 2003).

[66] N. Akizuki, "Sekai Chitsujo no Henyo to Kokka: 'Mankoku Hoho no Juyo to Chuka Shisutemu: Kai Chitsujo no Kyokai kara Kokusai Hoteki na Kokkyo e:' Chosen to Shi no Kyokai Chitai o meguru Kenkyushi" [Acceptance of International Law in East Asia: Modernization, Sovereign State, and a Traditional Order], Meiji Gakuin Daigaku Kokusai Gakubu Fuzoku Kenkyujo Nenpo, 13: 5–6.

which he believes will characterize Sino-Japanese relations. He argues that the Changbai/Paekdu issue bodes well for Japan, insofar as it should smooth the way for closer Japanese–Korean friendship, forged in opposition to China.[67]

One suspects that Nakanishi has gained a little more traction with his essay than has Akizuki with his strictly academic text. One Japanese blogger has registered incredulity with South Korea's claim over Changbai/Paekdu Mountain. He notes two points. First, North Korea maintains near silence over the issue. Second, Changbai/Paekdu Mountain is physically very far removed from South Korean territory. He argued that South Korea had "unilaterally" created this problem, and contrasts the South Korean stance with that of North Korea's "silence". This silence he attributes to the fact that China is North Korea's only "lifeline", and that North Korea feels utterly unable to "complain" to China. He concludes that Japan should "learn" from China, and come out strongly against South Korean attempts to change the name of the Sea of Japan.[68]

Another Japanese netizen has registered his surprise at this territorial dispute. He acknowledged that he had long since known of a widespread Chinese "backlash" against the Koreans. In this regard, he pointed to a Chinese conception of the Koreans as having failed to develop their own culture and having simply "stolen" Chinese culture. He regarded the Changbai/Paekdu issue as evidence that Sino-Korean disputes go beyond the cultural realm and also include territorial problems.[69]

Many Japanese bloggers tend to view the Changbai/Paekdu issue through the prism of territorial issues that involve Japan. One has asked whether any "demonstration movements" (similar to those which bedevil Sino-Japanese relations) have arisen in China over the Changbai/Paekdu issue. Another concludes that the Chinese "make their own maps" and

[67]T. Nakanishi Terumasa, Semarikuru Ni-Chu Reisen no Jidai: Nihon wa Daigi no Hata o Kakageyo [*The Impending Era of Sino-Japanese Cold War: Fly the Flag, Japan!*] (Tokyo: PHP Shinsho, 2013).

[68]"Kita Chosen Mondai", February 3, 2007. Available at: http://blogs.yahoo.co.jp/shiraty5027/28183999.html.

[69]"Kyo no Burogu: Chūgoku no Ken-Kan Kanjo, Senryo Mondai mo Riyu Hitotsu?", February 26, 2009. Available at: http://news.searchina.ne.jp/disp.cgi?y=2009&d=0226&f=column_0226_005.shtml.

therefore dispute territory with virtually all of their neighbors, including Japan. Yet another states simply that the Chinese are the "same as a band of robbers". Having read these (and other) comments, another blogger concluded that China is bent on expansion, then veered away from the Changbai/Paekdu issue to note that Chinese citizens living in Japan may well be "preparing for an internal [Japanese] revolt" which would presumably assist China in its claims over the Senkaku Islands and even Okinawa Prefecture.[70]

Conclusions

Japan and South Korea are both wealthy industrial powerhouses that have much more in common with each other than with China, and are both strategically allied with the US. Yet, although the political establishments in both countries might see China as a constant threat, Korea and Japan still popularly view each other with suspicion. By contrast, popular perceptions of the China threat in either country can be swayed by escalation of territorial disputes these two allies still have with one another. In that sense, it is hardly surprising that the famous rapport between President George W. Bush and Prime Minister Junichiro Koizumi worked to embolden Japanese "nationalists and reactionaries" much to the chagrin of *both* the South Korean and Chinese leadership.[71]

In the realm of popular sentiment, Korea's ongoing historical and territorial disputes with both China and Japan disallows clear-cut solidarity with either party, or explicit analogies with the dispute between China and Japan, because both powers are regarded as being dangerous to South Korea, and not trusted by any means. The escalation of the Japan–China dispute in 2012, which immediately followed South Korea's most recent spat with Japan over Tokdo, temporarily led to more positive public opinion toward China, but quickly gave way to more balanced analysis of the issue. If the dispute was to recur now in the midst of North Korea's threats

[70]"Yahoo! Japan Chiebukuro", September 19, 2012. Available at: http://detail.chiebukuro.yahoo.co.jp/qa/question_detail/q1094339390.

[71]K. E. Calder, "Critical Junctures and the Contours of Northeast Asian Regionalism", in *ibid.* and F. Fukuyama (eds.), *East Asian Multilateralism: Prospects for Regional Stability* (Baltimore: Johns Hopkins University Press), pp. 15–39.

against South Korea and China's continued reluctance to rein in its "client" state, a fact (or rather perception that North Korea is merely a "vassal" or worse a "puppet" of China) which also pricks the nationalist pride of many South Koreans, support for Chinese claims would likely be ambiguous. The academic community and policy-making elite in South Korea favor aligning Korea with the US and Japan against Chinese naval expansion in the East and South China Seas. However, deep political divisions between the political left (which favors China and North Korea) and the right (which favor the US and Japan) and the continuing question of Tokdo are likely to prevent South Korea from effectively coordinating a common response with Japan against China in the foreseeable future.

Similarly, in view of the Takshima/Tokdo dispute — Japanese bloggers hardly spare South Korea in their analysis of the dispute over Socotra Rock. Their respective alliance with the USA notwithstanding, many Japanese appear concerned about rapprochement between China and South Korea. However, others in Japan's far right might actually revel in escalation of the Socotra or Changbaishan disputes as a form of teaching South Korea a "lesson" in middle power hubris. And in the background lingers much phobia about putative Chinese designs on Okinawa or mainland Korea, putative Korean designs on China's Northeast, and bitter memories of Japan's wartime brutality. While identifying popular suspicion and resentment in Northeast Asia is a confirmatory finding, one issue this chapter points to that deserves further attention is growing unease about South Korea's delicate balancing act in the face of China's rise. Economically (and culturally) close to China, and quite often at loggerheads with Japan, South Korea's experience of the 1980s–1990s is highly germane to China's ongoing reforms. It is also a US ally whose conduct as a middle power is important to monitor in the context of deteriorating Sino-Japan relations and American re-balancing.

Chapter 7

Conclusions

The ongoing phenomenon, generally labeled "the rise of China", continues to amaze, disturb, and fascinate both the general public and academia across the globe. This book has sought to examine the various effects and perceptions of China's precipitous rise to global power in the West, in China itself, in Korea and in Japan.

The book began with an examination of the attempts in academia to contextualize China's current rise within the framework of economic history. Western European and American supremacy, economic and technological, was arguably the accepted "truth" of the past 200 years. During these centuries of Western preeminence, a Eurocentric dichotomy was constructed between the "advanced West" and the "backward East" in intellectual circles to rationalize and legitimize in historical, cultural, and economic terms the "superiority of the West".[1] With the rise of China in the late 20th and early 21st centuries, however, it is possible to detect a shift away from this Eurocentric Western model, an attempt to rethink East–West binaries and question the validity and durability of Western economic and technological supremacy. No longer is Western hegemony considered a perpetual phenomenon or even a palpable reality before the late 18th century among global historians, world historians, and economic historians.

The pre-1700s global order in which China stood on a par with or excelled in many ways the capacities of its Western counterparts is consequently receiving renewed consideration and scrutiny. The two

[1] See E. Said, *Orientalism* (New York, Vintage Books, 1971) for a full treatment. For revisionist critique of some of Said's assertions see R. Irwin, *For the Lust of Knowing: The Orientalists and their Enemies* (London, Penguin Books, 2006).

comparative studies examined in the first chapter, *Rome and China* and *Life Under Pressure*, to some extent exemplify these academic attempts to rationalize China's rapid rise by placing the phenomenon in historical context, presenting the rise as not so much a novelty, but merely a restoration of China's standing in the world and thereby confirming the rehabilitation of China in Western academic circles as a respectable and increasingly dominant player in the global order. Was there a great divergence that separated the West from China? If so, when did this occur? The debate continues, but that debate is now firmly based on the general assumption in the West that a point of convergence has finally been reached or is about to be reached by the West and China. The disparity in power between the West and China is no longer a lasting reality and this is faithfully reflected in current academic patterns of analysis.

How unique is today's "China Model"? Can it be defined and is it exportable? It was noted that the answers offered are varied and complex, ranging from a defense of the much-maligned Washington consensus and attempts to explain the "China Model" within that consensus to an enthusiastic argument for the propagation of the so-called "Beijing consensus" *in lieu* of the old Washington consensus. The essence of this debate however is, as can be expected, the specter of China posing a challenge to the current US global hegemony.

The arguments touched the essence of what exactly should constitute the "China Model". A neo-Maoist socialist model or a democratic or quasi-democratic neo-liberal model favored by liberals/neo-liberals in China and the West? Or as Zheng Yongnian argued is China's 30 years of reform to a great extent based on the pre-modern Chinese tenet of *zhongyong* and therefore is the "China Model" constrained by neither neo-Maoism nor neo-liberalism? Is China a "civilizational state"[2] rather than simply a "nation state" and therefore capable of avoiding the developmental precedents/models set by Western nations? What seems apparent is that neo-Maoism or socialism with Chinese characteristics even more than neo-liberalism has virtually no place in the new "China Model" being proposed by the majority of China's intellectuals and elite. The complexity of Chinese

[2]W. Zhang, *The China Wave: Rise of a Civilizational State* (Hackensack, NJ: World Century Publishing Corporation, 2012).

internal debate on the future trajectory of the "China Model" is noteworthy and its growing sophistication is revealed in the work of writers such as Yan Xuetong. It was observed how Yan Xuetong seeks to articulate China's moral claim to global leadership by drawing inspiration from China's ancient Classical literature and philosophy, particularly Xunzi. Yan boldly envisions a China-led global order under the aegis of China's virtuous *wangdao* (*in lieu* of the "aggressive" "hegemony" of the United States).

However, is the world prepared for the establishment of Chinese *wangdao* leadership? The possibility or eventuality of a China-led global order is arguably dependent not just on economic developments but also on the attitudes toward China of key regional players in the East Asia region, namely Korea and Japan. The litmus test for the world's readiness for the transition to Chinese leadership would naturally have to be taken in China's own regional setting in East Asia via the examination of the perceptions of China's immediate neighbors Korea and Japan of China's rapid rise. The episode of the renaming of South Korea's capital in Chinese was particularly instructive in this regard. It was observed how, officially, the PRC government reacted with prudence to the Korean requests for the name-change with little jingoism or attempts at confrontation.

Yet, just under the surface among the Chinese public a more militant, virulently nationalistic mood was also evident. Particularly disturbing was the derision in some (but not all) quarters of Chinese blogosphere: South Korea's requests for the name-change was depicted as a "revolt" and "impertinent self-assertion" of a former "vassal" state. Such militant nationalism,[3] if not carefully managed, could potentially jeopardize any chances of China staking a moral claim to leadership even in East Asia, let alone the wider world.

This is especially important when one takes into consideration the complexity of Korean perceptions of China. The fault-lines that divide Korean society and politics are still evident and the fear among Koreans (particularly those of right-wing leanings who are the majority and by inclination hostile to China) of an increasingly powerful China is often

[3]For a full detailed analysis of Chinese nationalism, see W. Zheng, *Never Forget National Humiliation: Historical Memory in Chinese Politics and Foreign Relations* (New York, Columbia University Press, 2012), esp. pp. 221–242.

very real and at time quite alarmist.[4] It would be in China's best interests to strengthen its supporters on the left of South Korea's political spectrum who are favorably inclined toward cooperation with China by adopting a more moderate and conciliatory policy toward Korea. Cooperation would only be secured if as in the case of the name-change, a new *modus operandi* of resolving bilateral disputes and ultimately securing closer relations is adopted to mitigate the equally fervent nationalistic feelings of Koreans vis-à-vis China.[5] Securing the cooperation of Korea becomes even more vital for China when one observes the evidence of Japan's growing anxiety over China's rise. The generally (though by no means uniformly) favorable Japanese response and even support for Korea's decision to assert its "independence" vis-à-vis China on the issue of the name-change arguably reflected the Japanese desire to maintain the current balance of power in East Asia, which would be disturbed if the Koreans were to shift their allegiance to China and sever ties with their American and Japanese allies.

The deeply ingrained mistrust among East Asian nations toward each other is clearly evident from the analysis of recent East Asian international relations and this may prove to be a daunting obstacle to China's aim to assume the leadership role in the region. At the heart of the mistrust and discord are the as-yet unresolved territorial disputes that continue to muddy popular and elite perceptions. It was observed that although Japan and South Korea have much more in common with each other than with China, are both strategically allied with the US, and the political establishments in both countries to a large extent see China as a foreseeable threat, Korea and

[4] *cf.* B.-R. Shin, "The Perspective of Tang Taizong towards the Three Eastern Kingdoms: Searching for the origins of the Northeast Project", in J. S. Lee and S. H. Jo (eds.), *Conflict in the Korean Peninsula and China's Intervention* (Seoul: Sunin, 2012), pp. 17–49; C. H. Park, "Crisis in North Korea and China's Military Intervention" in J. S. Lee and S. H. Jo (eds.), *Conflict in the Korean Peninsula and China's Intervention* (Seoul: Sunin, 2012), pp. 221–251; D.-H. Cha, *The US–China Rivalry over Naval Hegemony in East Asia: The Transfer of Naval Power Between the US and China with a Special Focus on the Attack on the Cheonam* (Seoul: Book Korea, 2012).

[5] For an excellent analysis of nationalism in East Asia and the distortion of history for nationalist agendas in all three East Asian states (China, Korea, and Japan), see S.-S. Yi, *Created Antiquity: The Early Modern Nation-State's Story of East Asia* (Seoul: Samin, 2001).

Japan still popularly view each other with a similar, if not the same level of suspicion with which they view China. Popular perceptions of the China threat in either country can be swayed by escalation of territorial disputes these two allies still have with one another. In the case of Korea, its ongoing historical and territorial disputes with both China and Japan disallows clear-cut solidarity with either party. Thus, the escalation of the Japan–China dispute in 2012, which immediately followed South Korea's most recent spat with Japan over Tokdo, temporarily led to more positive public opinion toward China, but quickly gave way to more balanced analysis of the issue.

The academic community and policy-making elite in South Korea instinctively favor aligning Korea with the US and Japan against possible Chinese naval expansion in the East and South China Seas and intervention in North Korea.[6] However, deep political divisions between the left (which favors China and North Korea) and the right (which favors the US and to a lesser degree Japan) and the continuing question of Tokdo are likely to prevent South Korea from effectively coordinating a common response with Japan against China in the foreseeable future. To a large extent, China's future as the new "leader" of East Asia and the wider world hinges on its ability to navigate successfully the treacherous waters of East Asian international relations and to win over the confidence of Korea and Japan, a daunting prospect even in the best of circumstances, but one that cannot be ignored by China if it truly aspires to become the next global superpower.

This current situation, as difficult as it already is for China, could be further complicated if and when North Korea collapses. How successfully or poorly China and the US manage an implosion of the Stalinist state will arguably determine which of the two powers will earn the lasting allegiance of the Korean people and thereby a firm geopolitical foothold in the Korean peninsula. That Korea's reunification could potentially cause a tectonic shift in the geopolitical landscape of East Asia was already noted by Brzezinski as early as 1997.[7] He warned that if Korea (united or divided) were to

[6]See J.-H. Yi, *China's Maritime Strategy* (Seoul: Gold Egg, 2007) and S.-H. Yi, "The Rise of China and the Response of the US: Security Implications for Korea", in J. S. Lee and S. H. Jo (eds.), *Conflict in the Korean Peninsula and China's Intervention* (Seoul: Sunin, 2012), pp. 253–286.

[7]Z. Brzezinski, *The Grand Chessboard: American Primacy and its Geostrategic Imperatives* (New York: Basic Books, 1997), p. 157.

align itself with China, Japan would then feel obliged to rearm and go nuclear and that this could then potentially lead to the disappearance of the rationale for the maintenance of the US security umbrella in East Asia, i.e., it could lead to the end of US geopolitical influence in the region.[8] Naturally, if China wishes to become a global power, this is exactly the scenario that China should aim for, a pro-China Korea and a Japan that due to the economic and geopolitical necessity created by the Sino-Korean alliance, accepts membership in a new China-led regional order. Obviously for Washington, this is exactly the outcome to avoid.

The recent diplomatic charm offensive launched by Xi Jinping to woo South Korea's conservative president Park Geun-hye is an indication that the current administration in Beijing is to a certain extent conscious of this geopolitical situation. North Korea is bound to fail at some point (arguably, it already has) and the Korea that follows the collapse of the Kim dynasty will in all likelihood be a greater South Korea, not a federation in which North Korea retains its identity or a Chinese-controlled puppet state feared by some South Korean analysts.[9] Yet Beijing's continuing support of North Korea (arguably on the basis of outdated geopolitical concerns of the Cold War) and its revisionist stance on historical matters such as Goguryeo and Balhae (Bohai) disputes are linked in the popular perception to territorial claims. These may re-fuel resentment in South Korea toward Chinese "interference" and "arrogance", opening up avenues for the US to exploit anti-Chinese sentiments in South Korea and strengthen the case for the preservation of the US–South Korea military alliance even after Korean reunification.

If China wishes to achieve leadership status in East Asia, it must remove the rationale for the maintenance of US troops on the Korean peninsula, which simply cannot be achieved if South Koreans have legitimate reasons to fear Chinese intentions toward North Korean territory and the peninsula as a whole. Washington has so far proved inept in exploiting the residual Cold-War-era "sinophobia" amongst South Korea's conservative military

---

[8]Z. Brzezinski (1997), pp. 169, 171, 190–191.

[9]C. H. Park, "Crisis in North Korea and China's Military Intervention", in J. S. Lee and S. H. Jo (eds.), *Conflict in the Korean Peninsula and China's Intervention* (Seoul: Sunin, 2012), pp. 221–251.

establishment. If the US truly wishes to maintain its hegemony in East Asia, it must do more to underscore Korean resentment of Chinese "interference" in the Korean peninsula and magnify the scope of Chinese ambitions toward Korea in the minds of the Korean public by persistent propaganda and charm offensives highlighting the benefits of the US–Korea alliance: security guarantees against Chinese and even Japanese "aggression".

It must also do more to appeal to Korean nationalists. The South Korean left did so in the past in order to rouse anti-American feelings, but such stratagem could just as easily be used by the right to ignite anti-Chinese sentiments.[10] In the case of China, the options are clear: (1) keep on supporting the failed Kim regime in the North and earn the lasting enmity of the eventual rulers of the peninsula (that is the south) and thereby destroy any chances of creating a Korea that is favorably inclined toward Chinese leadership; (2) more logically, sever ties with the decrepit North, gravitate more firmly toward South Korea, stop the useless battle over ancient history, and thereby convince the South Koreans that the US presence in Korea is not a necessity; (3) go one step further by stopping the saber rattling in the East and South China Seas which is instilling fear of China in all East Asian nations and pushing them into closer cooperation with the US.

The struggle for global supremacy between the US and China has arguably already commenced in East Asia. Whether China will emerge out of it as a superpower to rival the US or merely another Japan will depend heavily on how well its leaders manage the geopolitical situation in East Asia. The verdict so far is mixed. China has so far alienated many in the region with seemingly little gains.[11] But, as we explained, it could also launch periodic "charm offensives" and offer concessions in a bid to drive a wedge between South Korea, the US, and Japan. Whether the Chinese leadership can learn from their mistakes and adapt with greater skill to the shifting geopolitical realities of the East Asian region remains to be seen. Superpower or bust? History will eventually tell the story.

---

[10]The potential for which can clearly be seen in the polls: J.-H. Jeong, *The Rise of China and the Future of the Korean Peninsula* (Seoul: Seoul National University Press, 2011), pp. 334, 376.

[11]*cf.* the views of E. N. Luttwak, *The Rise of China vs. the Logic of Strategy* (Cambridge MA; London: The Belknap Press of Harvard University Press, 2012), whose opinions concerning Chinese geostrategic errors are rather extreme, but still worth consideration.

Index